BELGIAN ARCHITECTURE
BEYOND BELGIUM

A+**editions**

The preliminary question naturally concerns the very definition of the subject itself. What, ultimately, are we exporting when we talk about the export of Belgian architecture on the international stage? This question was raised on the occasion of a one-day round-table discussion. Each of the participants to the discussion was involved, in his or her own way, in the export of Belgian architecture: architects, academics, property developers, and government agency delegates working in the field of export support. The essential points of this exchange are included in the section entitled 'Around the table'. It soon emerged from the discussion that architecture is not a clearly defined product, but a practice. On the other hand, it also transpired that architecture cannot merely be considered a purely technical issue and that firms with an eye for the cultural component of their designs score at least as well in terms of export thanks to the strong profile of their content and methodology. The challenge in defining such a subject underlines the complexity involved in its export, and especially the question of export support in Belgium, which is, it seems, still in its early stages when compared to the situation in neighbouring countries, although an enthusiastic dynamic is already in place.

Is there a Belgian specificity to the export of architecture?

Another question worth asking is that of the Belgian specificity of exporting architecture, and thus the question as to whether it implies the export of a certain practice of architecture, or the figure of the architects themselves? In his introduction to this special issue, the Ghent-based academic Johan Lagae traces the development in this field from the 19th century onwards, and raises the question as to whether it is 'a story of big names'. Indeed, Belgian architecture on the international stage has so far never involved major names launched abroad with the support of government authorities. The same conclusion was drawn during the part of the round-table discussion entitled 'Around the table': "Our export product is our

know-how rather than a specific style". The underlying explanation for this phenomenon is rather complex. It is true that Belgian architects rarely make any grand gestures in their work and that they prefer to remain focused on the essential. At the same time, however, there is no denying that Belgians rarely identify with their architecture, on the one hand, and that politicians, on the other, have failed to discern the real potential of this difficultly identifiable matter, certainly over the last 30 years. It nevertheless remains that Belgian architects who try to stretch their wings beyond their national borders rely on themselves and their networks, whether they be economic, cultural, academic, or personal. The decision to work abroad is due, for some, to a willingness to diversify the firm's portfolio so as to increase turnover, while for others, export can represent an opportunity to have access to challenging commissions or can be a way out of a saturated national market. For what lies at the root of the Belgian export of architecture is first and foremost an obvious fact, and that is, that as a small country, our attention has always been turned outwards. It is a no less obvious fact that also explains another specificity of Belgian architecture: the tendency to explore the potential that is found abroad and combine it with Belgian technical mastery rather than implement a 'Belgian' project on foreign soil. This consideration for the native culture can be integrated either through the client or through a local architectural firm, which it seems inevitable to associate with to successfully complete a project on the international stage. Some partners thus have a particular know-how, while others are intimately familiar with the local building culture and red tape.

Views from abroad

In an attempt to reverse our perspective and detect what drives foreigners to call on Belgian architects and engineers, we decided to put a number of questions to the editors in chief of international reviews that publish regularly on Belgian projects. What viewpoint do they

Carrying out an assessment of the export of Belgian architecture is no easy thing. There are no statistics on the subject, and neither, it seems, are there any publications that deal with this topic. Belgian Architecture Beyond Belgium, a special issue of A+ Belgian Review of Architecture, aims to provide a brief overview of the situation. To do so, several aspects of this topic will be highlighted.

have on Belgian architectural production? What, if any, is Belgian architecture's input regarding the architecture of their country? What are its highlights, its characteristics? Their opinions are included in the section entitled 'Views from abroad'. Besides representing individual personalities, their answers reveal a culture that is specific to each of the countries where the review in question is published. A specific cultural and historical background emerges in view of the relations these countries have had and still have with Belgium.

What are Belgian architects producing abroad?

These six perspectives also highlight the fact that while Belgian architectural production is widely known and recognized, Belgian architectural production abroad is much less so. Perhaps this is due to the fact that the projects conducted outside Belgium represent at most 50% of the production of Belgian firms and that a firm's reputation overwhelmingly relies on the bulk of its portfolio. The publicization of these firms therefore mainly happens through what has been developed in Belgium. Belgian Architecture Beyond Belgium wishes to shed light on the specificities of work produced abroad and provide an overview of this production through a selection of 25 Belgian architectural firms. Each firm's key export project is thus analyzed in detail through interviews as well as photographs and plans. The selection is an attempt to show the formal diversity that is currently to be found in Belgian architecture abroad. The selection thus includes architectural firms of various sizes and which have either conducted a one-time operation on foreign soil or, on the contrary, are seeking to develop their foreign portfolio. It also includes firms which have built in Europe and/or the rest of the world; firms which have responded to direct commissions, to international competitions, or to invitations from non-governmental organizations; firms whose export enables them to highlight their very own expertise, or to tread new ground by taking on commissions of an entirely new nature or scale, commissions not usually

found in Belgium. It would indeed seem unlikely that a firm could here work on a plot measuring 155 hectares, build a winery, or set a villa atop an island cliff at an altitude of 159 metres above sea level.

Viewed as a whole, this ensemble of projects, which have either been completed since 2005 or are still ongoing, is illustrative of the gradual move towards a globalization of architecture. We may indeed be witnessing, as Johan Lagae writes, "the emergence of the first generation of Belgian architects that has opened its eyes to the whole world with no inhibitions and no prior agenda fixated on quick profits".

What will become of Belgian architecture beyond Belgium?

While the present issue knowingly chose to limit itself to observing and assessing the production of Belgian architects present on the international stage as 'architectural firms', it goes without saying that the export of Belgian architecture is a much wider phenomenon, and encompasses a range of projects and expertise that are the privilege of other entities such as consultancy firms and universities. The future of the export of Belgian architecture thus also belongs to many other actors. This future has been evoked on numerous occasions in this issue, and two characteristics tend to emerge. The first is that the future seems to belong to networks of smaller entities that are located in various countries and will work together occasionally or structurally. The second is that the next 30 years will increasingly involve a reciprocal learning process. In time, therefore, this might well lead to the disappearance of the notion of export.

Audrey Contesse
EDITOR IN CHIEF
A+ BELGIAN REVIEW OF ARCHITECTURE

Hardware.

BEGA

BEGA – Light outdoors.

PO Box 3160 · D-58689 Menden
Hennenbusch · D-58708 Menden
Germany
P +49 2373 966-0
F +49 2373 966-260
info@bega.com
www.bega.com

BEGA light design elements
Protection class IP 65
Discharge lamps
HIT-CE 35 W · 3600 Lumen

Software.

'FOREIGN AFFAIRS'.
ON 19TH- AND 20TH-CENTURY BELGIAN ARCHITECTS ABROAD

TEXT Johan Lagae

A story of big names?

In today's globalized context, it seems almost normal that every renowned Belgian architectural firm should not only be working in Belgium, but also designing and building projects abroad. The question arises as to how new this phenomenon is. How 'international' was the portfolio of the architects who make up the Belgian architectural canon? Although no in-depth research has been done on this topic, an initial glance at the oeuvres of leading 19th- and 20th-century Belgian architects shows that the number of projects they worked on abroad is small and amounts to no more than the occasional building. It is true that Henry Van de Velde built some notable works in Germany and the Netherlands, and that from the 1990s onwards the later generation, including bOb van Reeth and Charles Vandenhove, also has a number of buildings in the surrounding countries to their name. But Victor Horta's achievements abroad are limited to the castle at Chambley in France and the Grand Bazaar department store in Frankfurt (1903-05), both of which have, however, been destroyed. Even Victor Bourgeois, who, as the first chairman of the CIAM, possibly had the highest international profile of all Belgian 'masters of modern architecture', only built projects outside Belgium in connection with exhibitions. The house he built for Dr Boll in Stuttgart, for instance, was in the context of the Weissenhof Estate (1927).

So there is no figure like Le Corbusier in Belgian architectural history, someone "whose wanderings", as the architectural historian Jean-Louis Cohen once aptly put it, "are surpassed only by those of Tintin" and for whom the whole world was a potential workplace. The absence of big names on the Belgian architectural scene from the building sites of the world contrasts sharply with the prominent position Belgian engineers and construction companies have occupied there. During the interwar years, Edgard Frankignoul successfully marketed the Franki piles as an effective foundation system with applications from Vatican City to Kiev and Hong Kong,

while the Ghent-born engineer and professor Gustave Magnel developed an internationally renowned cement-research laboratory at Ghent University. Yet there remains indeed a history to be written about Belgian architects who have been active abroad. But then we have to turn our attention to people who usually go unnoticed in standard histories of Belgian architecture. In addition, there is little purpose in constructing this sort of story in a conventional way around any individual designer. It would seem more useful to tell the story on the basis of a number of vectors that guided work abroad in the late 19th and 20th centuries: industrial expansion, missionary work, colonization, development aid, and globalization. What follows is an initial and of course incomplete attempt to tell this story.

Industrial expansion

From the second half of the 19th century onwards, many Belgian industrialists emerged as ambitious and internationally oriented, partly out of sheer necessity because of the limited domestic market. In addition to such concrete builders as the above Frankignoul, this applied in particular to the Belgian metal constructors who succeeded in selling their products in such remote tropical regions as Latin America, Africa and Asia. The Forges d'Aiseau exported prefabricated metal buildings to Mexico, Brazil, Chile and the Congo (fig. 1). The Baume-Marpent company built up a market that was well spread out internationally and even continued after the Second World War. The activities of the Belgian industrialists created opportunities for Belgian architects. Around 1919, for example, Lucien François built several notable villas in Sicily for the Italian-Belgian company Les Tramways de Palerme. The historian Eddy Stols was the first to point out the striking but little-known Belgian impact on the architecture of the Argentine capital Buenos Aires from the second half of the 19th century onwards. As from 1870, Julien Dormael (1846-1924) built up a lucrative career there putting up prestigious

Although a full history of Belgian architecture remains to be written, Johan Lagae sheds some light on architects who were active on the international stage, yet who largely go unnoticed in conventional histories of Belgian architecture.

Beaux-Arts projects, while Henri Derée and Eugène Dhuicque later erected a monumental electric power station there (1924-28) as part of the work on the harbour under Belgian supervision (fig. 2).

A project that has been studied more thoroughly is the building of the 'Belgian' garden district Heliopolis on the outskirts of Cairo from 1905 onwards, an initiative of Edouard Empain, who had made his fortune and reputation with the worldwide laying of tramlines and the construction of the Paris metro. Empain recruited several architects to achieve his dream of a new town as an oasis in the desert. In addition to the French architect Alexandre Marcel, who had also created buildings for Leopold II, the main contributor was the still young Ernest Jasper, who worked for Empain in Heliopolis from 1907 to 1916, and notably designed the imposing Heliopolis Palace, "the most sumptuous hotel of the Orient". In 1927 Empain once again joined forces with Jasper to develop a tourist resort focusing on the exploration of nature in the Congolese town of Goma, but this was never completed given the economic crisis and Empain's death. Not long afterwards, Empain's son Louis followed in his father's footsteps and commissioned one of the leading figures of Belgian art deco, Antoine Courtens, to design a luxury leisure resort called Domaine de l'Estérel (1936-37) near Quebec in Canada (fig. 3). Courtens used a broad range of styles there, from modernist-inspired buildings to 'log cabins' inspired by the authentic originals. In the 1950s, Courtens also designed several more garden districts in France and Italy for the Empain group.

Belgian companies and entrepreneurs continued to seek out distant markets in the postwar period, too. Belgian participation in world exhibitions, often designed by Belgian architects, were an important channel for promotion and networking. Belgian pavilions at international trade fairs, although less well known, were no less important and sometimes gave young architects the opportunity to carry out

fig. 1
Church made out of prefabricated metal parts produced by the Forges d'Aiseau and built in Boma, Congo, 1899

© JOHAN LAGAE

'FOREIGN AFFAIRS'.
ON 19TH- AND 20TH-CENTURY BELGIAN ARCHITECTS ABROAD

↑ *fig. 2*
Henri Derée and Eugène Dhuicque, Electric power station, Buenos Aires, 1924-28

→ *fig. 3*
Antoine Courtens, Hôtel de la Pointe Bleue, Domaine de l'Estérel, Quebec, 1936

↑ *fig. 5*
Alphonse de Moerloose, 'Twin churches' of Gaojiayingzi (above) and Shebiya (below) just after completion, 1903-04

← *fig. 4*
Lucien Engels, Belgian pavilion for the trade fair in Lagos, Nigeria, 1962 (reused two years later for the fair in Casablanca, Morocco)

© ARCHIVES D'ARCHITECTURE MODERNE | BRUSSELS

© KADOC-KULEUVEN – FOTOCOLLECTIE SCHEUT

© MIL DE KOONING

THE MISSIONARY ZEAL OF THE CATHOLIC
CHURCH WAS ANOTHER MAJOR VECTOR IN THE
INTERNATIONAL DISSEMINATION OF BELGIAN
DESIGN AND BUILDING EXPERTISE.

architectural experiments. Examples include Lucien
Engels' designs for the trade fairs in the Iraqi capital
Baghdad (1958) and the Nigerian capital Lagos (1962)
(fig. 4), as well as Jacques Dolphyn's pavilion at the
Rand Easter Show in Johannesburg (1962). Marcel Mignot
even concentrated the bulk of his work on this sort of
brief, and between 1965 and 1990 designed pavilions
for trade fairs from Hamburg to Poznan, Moscow,
Vancouver and Tehran.

Missionary work

In addition to the trading instincts of the Belgian
entrepreneurs, the missionary zeal of the Catholic church
was another major vector in the international dissemination of Belgian design and building expertise. From
the very first wave of missionaries in the 16th and 17th
centuries we find traces overseas of Flemish contributions
to the building of missionary posts and churches in
Latin America. But it was above all from the second half
of the 19th century that missionaries spread out deep
into Africa and Asia. Belgian companies responded to
this by developing a wide range of prefabricated metal
construction elements that could be used in church-
building, too. But in many cases the mission congre-
gations themselves took charge of making the hardware
needed for their missionary activities, often copying the
mother country. Thomas Coomans recently documented
the remarkable spread of St Luke Gothic in certain regions
of China in the early 20th century, based on a study
of the churches built by the missionary and architect
Alphonse de Moerloose (fig. 5).

In the Congo, which because of the colonial context
occupies a special position in the history of Belgian
missionaries, a very sizeable building heritage took
shape, often erected by local communities under the
leadership of a builder-friar. While the vast majority of
the buildings were primarily functional and quite modest,
other, more prestigious complexes were also built, often
using plans sent out by Belgian architects. As early as

1919, for example, Jos Vierin drew up a design for the
cathedral in Lubumbashi, while around 1950 Julien De
Ridder designed the plans for the churches in Beni and
Bingi. The debate on church architecture that took place
in Belgium between the wars also had repercussions in
the Congo (albeit of a limited nature), partly as a result
of Huib Hoste's articles in mission periodicals. Sometimes
exceptional ties were formed between architect and
client, as in the case of Roger Bastin, who initially was
approached to build a chapel for the Jesuit priest Léon
Verwilghen in Nyanza in Rwanda, but ended up designing
an imposing college complex, a girls' school and part of
the University of Burundi in Bujumbura (fig. 6). After the
Second World War, Henri Lacoste, the author of the most
imaginative Congo pavilion of the world exhibitions of
the 1930s, designed several religious buildings (churches,
seminaries, colleges, etc.) for Central Africa, several at the
request of his son, who worked there for the missionary
congregation of the White Fathers.

The story of the missionaries did not in fact end
with independence. In the 1960s the African church
was, after all, looking for a new identity. Architecture
was an important instrument in this process, and in the
absence of African architects, European designers played
a significant role. Paul Dequeker, a Belgian architect and
member of the Congregation of the Immaculate Heart of
Mary, who had taken a course in tropical architecture at
the AA school in London, built an exceptional number of
buildings in the Congo between 1959 and 1993 (churches,
schools, seminaries, model dwellings, etc.), which, as well
as taking account of the climate, also responded to the
local, often limited means of construction. His ideas still
form the basis of the training of Congolese architects
today. Lucien Kroll was no less active in this field. In
1968, for instance, he built an abbey for Benedictines
near Butare, and in that same year he also pleaded for
a locally embedded approach to the question of church
construction in Rwanda, in which his fascination for
participation makes itself felt.

'FOREIGN AFFAIRS'.
ON 19TH- AND 20TH-CENTURY BELGIAN ARCHITECTS ABROAD

© PHOTO ARCHIVES ROGER BASTIN/SOFAM

fig. 6
**Roger Bastin,
Collège du
Saint-Esprit,
Bujumbura, Burundi,
1952–61**

Colonization

When a huge piece of land in the centre of the African continent came into Belgian hands at the initiative of King Leopold II, it seemed the ideal opportunity to export Belgian architecture. Yet here too the story is more complex, and those who made a significant contribution were not in the first place professional architects, let alone the big names of Belgian architectural history. In the late 19th century, colonial officials in any case considered architects to be an unnecessary luxury. At the end of the 1920s, Raymond Cloquet, one of the first to settle as an independent architect in the Congo, found that the other players in the world of colonial building still considered the architect to be a 'parasite'. Anyway, Belgian architects initially showed little interest in expanding their activities overseas. When, in 1911,

the architectural periodical Tekhné warned that the development of Elisabethville (now Lubumbashi) was in danger of becoming a business for 'foreigners', specifically Greeks, Italians and Portuguese, there was barely any response to its call to Belgian colleagues to concern themselves with the problems of colonial building. The competition for the most important public building in the colony, the new residence for the governor-general in Leopoldville (now Kinshasa), which was held in 1928, also only elicited 12 entries, with Henri Lacoste, Raymond Moenaert and Léon Stynen being the better known participants. The fact that Raphael Verwilghen's very promising 1928-29 urban planning mission to the Kivu region fizzled out led to the modernist camp in the Belgian architectural milieu giving up the colony as a potential work area for a long time.

© PHOTO ARCHIVES ROGER BASTIN/SOFAM

Despite all this, some quite distinguished architecture was built in the Congo, especially as from the second half of the 1920s, mostly designed by people who have still not been given a place in the canon of Belgian architecture. In addition to Raymond Cloquet, there was also Henri Jordan and Richard Lequy, who occupied prominent positions in local public works departments. As from the 1930s, René Schoentjes, who for a long time had monitored the building policy in the colony for the Ministry of the Colonies in Brussels, concentrated on a career in colonial building and shortly after the Second World War built several exceptional school complexes. The real boom only took place from the early 1950s, when the colonial economy picked up, a ten-year plan was launched, and Brussels property firms and building contractors discovered that the colonial urban centres were a lucrative terrain. It was at that time that a series of Brussels architects started to expand their field of action to include the Congo: Maurice Houyoux, Marcel Lambrichs, Claude Laurens, Georges Ricquier, and others (fig. 7).

Even so, the number of architects residing in the colony in the 1950s remained limited, probably in part because the profession was not protected in the colony as it was at home. The majority of 'colonists-architects' worked for colonial companies or for the government and associated bodies. In addition to the Public Works Department, there were, for example, the Office des Transports au Congo (Otraco) and the Office des Cités Africaines (OCA), which in the 1950s built notable new neighbourhoods for Africans. Because a large part of this production did not appear in professional journals, many buildings have so far largely gone unnoticed. Thanks to archive research in the Congo, we know, for example, that Jacques Délire, Otraco's head architect, was the designer of the striking passenger harbour in Kinshasa (1956-59) (fig. 8). The work of Marcel Molleman, who collaborated with the public works department in Stanleyville (now Kisangani), also remained unknown for a long time, even though his projects are among the most notable modernist

buildings in that city. He was, for example, responsible for the fascinating design of the 1955 trade fair in Stanleyville, which is commonly attributed to Paul-Amaury Michel. In 1952, Maurice Heymans, who was initially the head of the urban planning department in Kinshasa, launched his own firm and built several blocks of flats along the capital's main boulevards.

Claude Strebelle stood out among the architects who resided in the Congo. He had conceived a love of Africa through his teacher Henri Lacoste, and started his career in the colony, first in the building department of the Union Minière du Haut Katanga and later, in 1953, established his own firm, Yenga, with Jean Leloup and André De Buyl. Several buildings which even now help define the urban landscape of Lubumbashi bear Strebelle's signature: the city's theatre, museum and music school, as well as several villas, a garage, a printing works, etc. (fig. 9). What's more, Strebelle endeavoured to create architecture related to the local vernacular architecture. It was no coincidence that he was also the artistic director of the art periodical Jeune Afrique, published in Elisabethville, which provided a forum for young Congolese artists. However, this sort of quest for a contemporary architecture rooted in the local architecture remained the exception. Postwar architecture in the Congo was in most cases a carbon copy of Western modernism, often designed by people who had never set foot in the Congo, but drew their inspiration from the buildings erected in Africa at the time, as illustrated in such professional journals as Rythme, l'Architecture d'Aujourd'hui and Architectural Review.

Development aid

The independence of the Congo did not bring about any radical break in the field of building. Many Belgian architects continued working there after 1960. Marcel Lambrichs, for example, built several banks and commercial complexes. But in the context of development aid, President Mobutu soon swapped Belgian for French expertise. From 1965 to 1975, a sizeable French urban-

TO CHART THE ROLE OF BELGIAN DESIGNERS,
WE HAVE TO ABANDON INDIVIDUALS AND
STUDY THE AS YET INACCESSIBLE ARCHIVES OF
BUILDING CONTRACTORS AND PLAYERS IN THE
PROPERTY SECTOR.

© MARC GEMOETS

fig. 7
Kinshasa, Boulevard
du 30 juin, featuring
(left) two residential
towers for Sabena
designed by Claude
Laurens (1952–54)
and (right) the com-
plex Le Royal, built by
the building contrac-
tors Trenteseaux–De
Smet after plans by
Délépine (1955)

fig. 8
Jacques Délire,
Passenger harbour,
Kinshasa, Congo,
1956–59

© MARC GEMOETS

'FOREIGN AFFAIRS'.
ON 19TH- AND 20TH-CENTURY BELGIAN ARCHITECTS ABROAD

← fig. 11
Georges Patfoort, Proposal for a village of 60 housing units on the basis of the 'habipat' principle

© ARCHIVES PATFOORT

↙ fig. 9
Claude Strebelle, Bâtiment du 30 juin (formerly a theatre), Lubumbashi, Congo, 1953-56

↓ fig. 10
Eugenio Palumbo, Faculty of Engineering, University of Lubumbashi, Lubumbashi, Congo, 1966

© JOHAN LAGAE

© JOHAN LAGAE

THE ABSENCE OF BIG NAMES ON THE BELGIAN
ARCHITECTURAL SCENE FROM THE BUILDING
SITES OF THE WORLD CONTRASTS SHARPLY
WITH THE PROMINENT POSITION BELGIAN
ENGINEERS AND CONSTRUCTION COMPANIES
HAVE OCCUPIED THERE.

planning mission was at work in Kinshasa, and French architects built some imposing complexes. Belgians were also pushed out of the market by other players. It was an architect of Italian origin, Eugenio Palumbo, who supervised the extensive school building programme for Unesco in the 1960s, though he later opened an office in Brussels too (fig. 10). Belgian architects then shifted their activities to other developing countries in Africa and Asia. It is striking how well former students of the La Cambre school of architecture are represented in this field. Pierre Humblet and Jan Maes, both former OCA architects in the Congo, specialized in hospital architecture and worked in several African countries; CERAU, a firm whose partners included Françoise Blomme and Roger Thirion, operated in Algeria, Nigeria, Rwanda, Cameroon and Colombia; Marc Gossé started a career as a technical volunteer in Algeria, designed projects for Iraq and, as a lecturer in 'Architecture and Development', inspired generations of students. Slightly later, the University of Leuven also played a part in this field by setting up its postgraduate Human Settlements curriculum. Development aid goes hand in hand with specific building types. In addition to schools and hospitals it is largely concerned with cheap housing. From the 1970s onwards, it was in this niche in the building market that experiments were also carried out with such new building materials as plastic. A striking example of this is the 'habipat', which the Brussels University professor Georges Patfoort developed in fibre-reinforced plastic between 1967 and 1972 and with which, at the recommendation of the United Nations, prototype villages were built in Chile, the Congo, Cyprus, Upper Volta and Ecuador (fig. 11).

Globalization

It was in the post-independence years that the profile of a new kind of designer arose internationally, the so-called 'nomadic expert', who offered his services around the world. Even more than Le Corbusier had done, such people as Michel Ecochard and Constantin Doxiadis succeeded

in working their way up to prominent positions with a truly global field of action. By setting up an efficient, high-performance office structure, it was these architects rather than the big names of architectural history who succeeded in convincing numerous institutional clients to award them briefs. These encompassed prestigious projects that often formed part of a policy which several former colonies were pursuing, that of 'nation building': new capitals, parliament buildings, law courts and the like. But it also involved large-scale office and commercial complexes and even extensive tourist infrastructure that was intended to ensure the new position of these countries in an increasingly globalized world. To a certain extent, the Sozacom Tower that Claude Strebelle and André Jacqmain built in Kinshasa for the head office of the Congolese mining industry is exemplary of this sort of brief, although the architecture of the project is special because it shows an emphatic ambition to design a 'clearly African skyscraper' in reaction to the encroachment of a generic 'corporate modernism' (fig. 12).

We also see projects like this in the portfolio of other architects who had previously worked in the Congo, such as Marcel Lambrichs of the Tekhné group, and which took shape around a number of former OCA staff members. Nevertheless, globalization and new, emerging economies offered opportunities elsewhere, too. In the early 1980s Jean and André Polak discovered the building market in Saudi Arabia, while between 1984 and 2002 the Belgian firm Atelier d'Art Urbain built major hotel complexes in Istanbul, Cairo and Monaco. However, if we want to chart the role of Belgian designers in this increasingly globalized world, we shall once more have to abandon the individual designer and start the study rather in the as yet inaccessible archives of building contractors and players in the property sector. In this light, it would be worthwhile to study international groups such as Blaton and Besix, and also someone like the notorious Charlie De Pauw, who, among other things, joined forces with the above Eugenio Palumbo for a project in Togo. A study like this would at

'FOREIGN AFFAIRS'.
ON 19TH- AND 20TH-CENTURY BELGIAN ARCHITECTS ABROAD

the same time expose the relative nature of internationalization. After all, in recent decades it has chiefly been the logic of economics that has driven building operations abroad. In this regard it should come as no surprise that so much attention is being paid to India and China in architectural guilds in Belgium and elsewhere. At the same time, the recent international activities of young Belgian design firms seems to suggest that other factors now play a part, too. It seems that we are witnessing today the first generation of Belgian architects that has fully opened its eyes to the whole world with no inhibitions nor prior agenda fixated on quick profits.

© MARC GEMOETS

fig. 12
Claude Strebelle and André Jacqmain, Sozacom Tower, Kinshasa, Congo, 1969-77

Bibliographic note
· *Anne Van Loo* **Repertorium van de architectuur in België van 1830 tot heden** – *Mercatorfonds | 2003*
· *Georges de Hens & V.-G. Martiny* **Académie Royale des Beaux-Arts de Bruxelles. Une école d'architecture. Des tendances 1766-1991** – *Brussels | 1992*
· *Paul-Emile Vincent (ed.)* **La Cambre a 60 ans** – *La Cambre | Brussels | 1987*
· *Maurice Culot et al.* **Archives d'Architecture Moderne. Catalogue des Collections, Tome I & II** – *AAM | Brussels | 1986 & 1999*
· *Anne Van Loo & Marie-Cécile Bruwier* **Heliopolis** *Mercatorfonds | Brussels | 2010*
· *Tom Avermaete* **De habipat. De plastiekexperimenten met 'self-help housing' van Georges Patfoort (1967-1984)** *in Tom Avermaete et al. (eds.)* **Wonen in Welvaart** *010 & VAI/CVAa | Rotterdam & Antwerp | 2006*
· *Maurice Culot & Anne-Marie Pirlot (eds.)* **Antoine Courtens. Créateur Art Deco** – *AAM | Brussels | 2002*
· *Johan Lagae* **'Kongo zoals het is'. Drie architectuur verhalen uit de Belgische kolonisatiegeschiedenis (1920-1960)** *3 volumes, unpublished doctoral thesis* – *Ghent University | 2002*
· *Eddy Stols & Rudy Bleys (eds.)* **Vlaanderen en Latijns-Amerika. 500 jaar confrontatie en métissage** – *Mercatorfonds | Antwerp | 1993*
· *Eddy Stols* **'De Belgen op de wereldwijde bouwwerf'** *pp.192-211 in Jacques Claes (ed.)* **De beschikbare ruimte. Reflecties over bouwen** *Lannoo | Tielt | 1990*

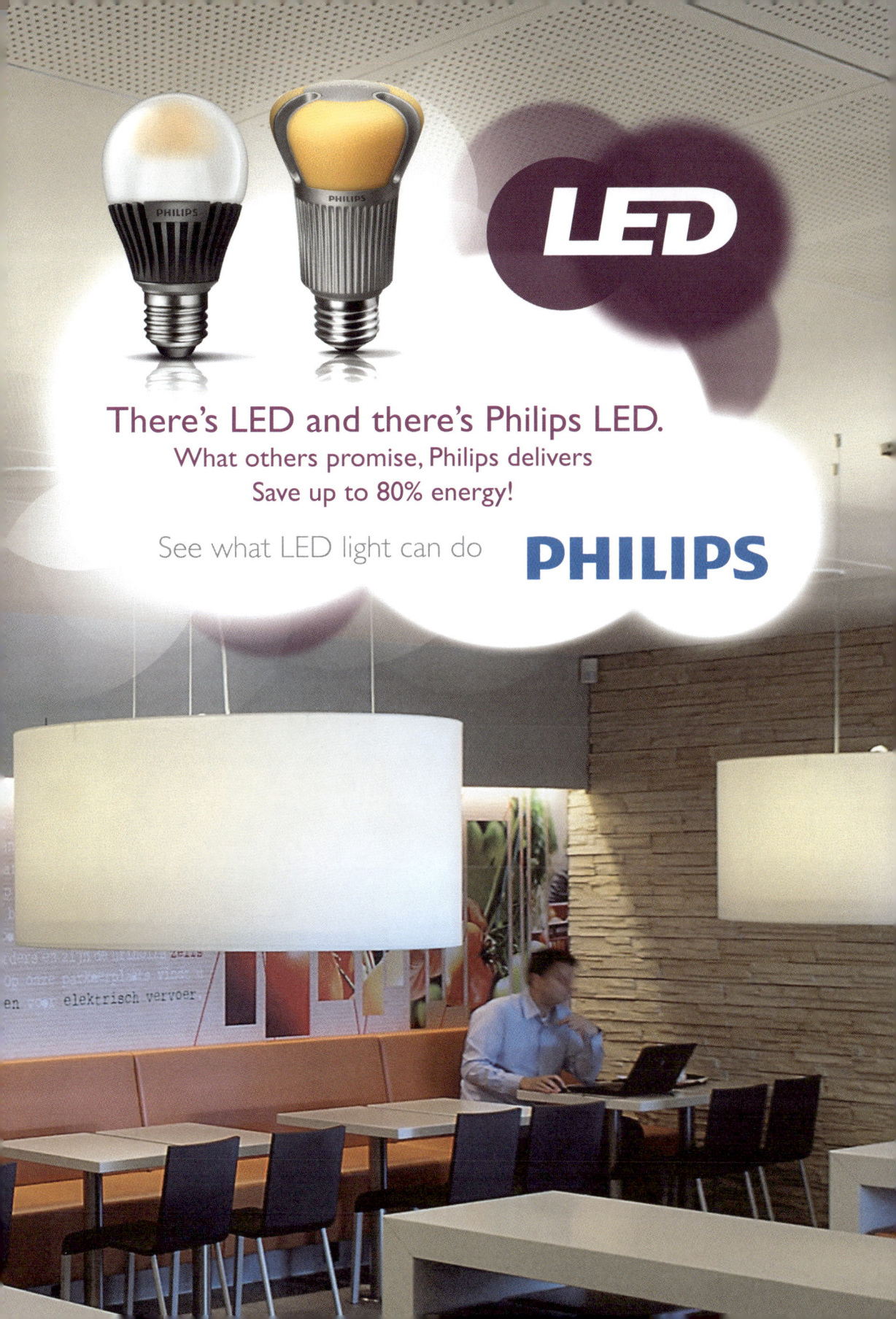

There's LED and there's Philips LED.
What others promise, Philips delivers
Save up to 80% energy!

See what LED light can do

AROUND THE TABLE

EXPORTING ARCHITECTURE OR ARCHITECTS?

EXPORTING ARCHITECTURE OR ARCHITECTS?

TEXT Pieter T'Jonck

The export of Belgian architecture was the topic of a one-day round-table discussion featuring several participants. How does it happen? Who is involved? What are the difficulties and opportunities? A first question is indeed whether, how and to what extent the authorities support the export of Belgian architecture. If so, does that support target individual firms, or does it involve the promotion of Belgian architecture as a whole? In other words, what, in fact, is being exported: architects, or a particular way of practising architecture? It soon transpired that architecture cannot merely be considered a purely technical issue. While virtually all participants in the discussion agree that the great professional expertise of Belgian architects is an important asset, it also seems that firms with an eye for the cultural component of their designs score at least as well in terms of export thanks to the strong profile of their content and methodology.

AUDREY CONTESSE I first wish to ask Carl Destoop and Aurore Boraczek about the current policy in both parts of the country in terms of export support in general, and export support for architecture in particular. The key question is whether that policy targets the export of architecture, or the export of (individual) architectural firms?

CARL DESTOOP I work for the FIT (Flanders Investment & Trade), a Flemish government agency. Our views on export have undergone a radical change. Everything used to revolve around trade, the sale abroad of goods produced in Flanders, but our approach has evolved over the last five years. We now think in terms of international enterprise. A good example is design. Designer products can be developed in Flanders, and this will create added value for Flanders. This does not necessarily mean, however, that these products will be made here. Production often takes place elsewhere. That is why we also offer support for the development of international partnerships. Applied to architecture, this could, for instance, mean facilitating partnerships with foreign firms.

PIETER T'JONCK Why this change from trade to enterprise or services?

CARL DESTOOP The delocalization of many companies was a decisive factor in this respect. Very little is still physically produced in our country. Added value comes especially from services, for example within the creative economy. But in order to obtain our backing, there must be some real added value for our country. We do not support traders, for instance.

PIETER T'JONCK What form does that support take when architecture is involved? Who or what do you support? And if you support individual architects, the question then is, how do you define who is to benefit from the support and how substantial that support is?

CARL DESTOOP Our primary mission is to support companies that want to operate at an international level. The initiative thus always comes from that side. We ourselves try not to define what the added value of Flemish architects or architecture could be. For that we largely rely on the VAi, the Flemish Architecture institute, just as we rely on Design Flanders for advice on design. We then do promotional work for those companies that came forward and that have passed a quality test.

AUDREY CONTESSE Is there a different policy on the French-speaking side?

AURORE BORACZEK Indeed. But perhaps we first need to recall that foreign trade has been regionalized in Belgium: Brussels Invest & Export (BI&E) represents Brussels, the AWEX represents Wallonia, and the FIT represents Flanders. A separate department was created in 2011 by Wallonia-Brussels International and the Wallonia-Brussels Federation in collaboration with the Brussels and Walloon Regions, and was entitled Wallonie-Bruxelles Architectures (WBA), just as had happened six years earlier for design. This was because we had noticed that each sector requires its own strategy. Distributing a film abroad is obviously not the same as exporting architecture. In one case it involves a clearly defined product, in the other, a practice. The particularity of the WBA is that it has cultural and economic competences. We are thus able to cover both aspects of what the term 'architecture' encompasses when organizing its promotion abroad.

AUDREY CONTESSE The support is still quite modest, however, if we compare the situation to our immediate neighbours, France and the Netherlands. France, for instance, has sent out large delegations of architects and academics to China to create an opening in the market there. That kind of attention for the export of services is much smaller here. Both the Netherlands and France also use their architecture to polish their reputation abroad. Can the same be said of Belgium?

CARL DESTOOP The idea that a creative product can contribute to a country's image is still quite new to us. We have traditionally been focused on large sectors such as the construction or clothing industries. They are easy to internationalize. Our service is somewhat ill suited for the creative industry. We rely on the VAi or on Design Flanders for advice in that field.

AURORE BORACZEK Unlike in France, say, Belgians rarely identify with their architecture. I've already written memos to some ministers to make clear to them that they are not making the most of these opportunities. If it involves fashion or design, they easily understand that there is a Belgian specificity, because they can immediately associate it with an image. But it remains difficult for architecture. That's why an energetic promotion of architecture must involve the valorization of the work performed here in Belgium. It is indispensable because it's not easy to explain the creative process underlying the construction of a building.

JÉRÔME MATTHIEU The problem, in my opinion, is that conducting a decent foreign policy is impossible given the huge dispersal of means. One will never develop sufficient clout this way. By contrast, every year at MIPIM (Marché International des Professionnels de l'Immobilier) the sector itself apparently manages to ensure its own self-promotion in a very convincing manner.

ISIDORE ZIELONKA That's not the only problem. In France, the government leads the way during export campaigns, and companies follow in its wake. In Belgium, companies have to beg the authorities to take the lead. And it still doesn't always happen. It's a question of mentality. The authorities in this country don't want to dirty their hands with commercial undertakings. Moreover, from a financial perspective, the support that is awarded represents little in relation to the efforts required to receive that support. In practice, if they wish to work abroad, architects will get a lot more out of tagging along with property developers.

AURORE BORACZEK Such missions do exist in Belgium: there are the crown prince's missions twice a year as well as the economic missions that open doors. In partnership with the FIT and BI&E we organized a mission to

Hong Kong earlier this year. Of course there are fewer missions than in France and less means, but it is our job to increase them.

HAN VERSCHURE Historically, however, this hasn't always been the case. In the late 19th and early 20th century, the authorities conducted promotional campaigns in countries like Russia, Ecuador and Brazil for large-scale infrastructure works. Architecture and engineering were a clear part of it. During the Brussels World's Fair in 1958, too, Belgian architecture was widely promoted. This policy has been neglected over the past 30 years, however. A minister-president like Kris Peeters is not interested in fields such as the environment, town planning or architecture, even though we have a lot of expertise in those very fields. He fails to understand the value of knowledge, and only has eyes for production. But if you fail to see what an incredible store of knowledge we have in this country, as in the field of building commissions, then you can't promote it. The current trend of thinking by sector shows a complete lack of vision.

FREEK PERSYN By contrast, the Dutch government, for instance, has a much smarter approach in this respect. We are currently involved in a commission for a new town-planning project for Istanbul. It was initiated through the International Architecture Biennale Rotterdam. This is a cultural organization, but it allows you to explore the situation on site and enables Dutch architects to play a significant role therein. That makes it possible to make the suitable arrangements for an enormous market.

PIETER T'JONCK Let's come back for a minute to the question of whether we are exporting architecture or architects.

OSWALD DELLICOUR We export experience and insight. As a small country our attention has, historically, always been turned outwards. But our export product is our know-how rather than a specific style. That is why foreigners come knocking on our door. How come? In the past a large and widely ramified network of Belgians took root in developing countries, notably thanks to the civil service system, which many young men chose instead of doing their military service. Their presence left a favourable impression and they often remained active later on. It is noticeable that there are Belgians at the highest levels of organizations such as the FAO who began their careers in this way. That network is now slowly dying out, given the abolition of the military service. For all that time, however, we were able to look after our own interests. The authorities hardly intervened, not even with a flyer. Their question was always the same: what are you selling?

JÉRÔME MATTHIEU But you do have something to sell. Belgian architects do wonders with tight budgets. They deliver high quality, taking into account the low exit prices or rent in Brussels. Indeed, due to those exit prices, Belgian architects rarely make any grand gestures. They're focused on the essential, and that's why, when a prestigious building is needed, clients tend to call in a foreign 'celebrity', which is not without risk, of course. I would thus be very curious to discover what Christian de Portzamparc's PUL project will become once he faces the economic constraints of our market – to be continued...

AUDREY CONTESSE Perhaps that is also due to the specificity of the curricula. It is easier for students in Belgium to take a degree in architectural engineering, whereas in France there is only one school which offers that possibility. Universities offer something more than Fine Arts Academies.

FREEK PERSYN I think you are narrowing down the issue too much if you limit the quality of Belgian architects to their ability to do a lot with a tight budget. The Jaspers firm is undoubtedly good at building, but it hardly cultivates the public and cultural aspects of its designs. They have built up no knowledge in that field. If that's how you define Belgian architecture, then you are exporting a narrow vision. Architecture is a physical product, but if you don't articulate its value then people won't be able to interpret it. That's the cultural aspect of architecture. American architecture cannot be interpreted in the same

IF YOU FAIL TO SEE WHAT AN INCREDIBLE STORE OF KNOWLEDGE WE HAVE IN THIS COUNTRY, THEN YOU CAN'T PROMOTE IT.

HAN VERSCHURE

way as Japanese architecture. Closer to home, you won't grasp the work of awg architecten if you have the wrong expectations about it. You have to make clear why you do what you do and what process you went through to get there. In other words, you have to enlighten your client.

CHRISTINE DE RUIJTER In this way you can also make clear to him what the value can be of using the same 'product'.

FREEK PERSYN We were able to build a high-rise in Albania because we were given an hour to explain how we wanted to approach the process, but also what result we were striving for. That's not the same as showing a few slides. If both these aspects, the cultural and economic, are artificially separated, then you face a huge problem in the case of export.

PIETER T'JONCK It strikes me that you use the term 'product' although you are emphasizing the cultural dimension. Isn't an architect primarily selling a way of thinking and an approach? Is 'product' the right term?

FREEK PERSYN I used that word so as to connect with people who, from their sector, have different expectations. A building is a product, but also a constellation of many other ideas and expectations, alliances, a certain openness, etc.

CARL DESTOOP That's not a story we can tell. For that we have to rely on others.

PIETER T'JONCK Freek Persyn is underlining the fact that architecture is something more than the mere accommodation of functions and that that's where its value lies. It's about what it brings to the world, not what it brings in, as Guy Châtel said.

PRUDENT DE WISPELAERE We always say: architecture begins when one has found the answers to everything else. Conversely, it's not because all the questions have been answered that one can talk of architecture. Architecture is an added value, the gift one contributes, often in spite of the client, or even without the client realizing it. Sometimes it's even a gift the architect gives on the sly, under the table.

ARCHITECTURE BEGINS WHEN ONE HAS FOUND THE ANSWERS TO EVERYTHING ELSE.

PRUDENT DE WISPELAERE

Light and insulation is in your hands.

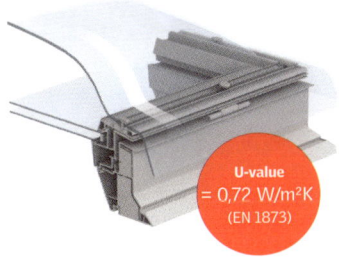

U-value = 0,72 W/m²K (EN 1873)

More info at velux.be

Feeling inspired? Recommend VELUX flat roof windows.

- Double glazed windows provide security and protection
- Optimal thermal and acoustic insulation
- Modern and elegant design
- Vented electric version

©2011 VELUX GROUP ®VELUX, HET VELUX LOGO, CABRIO, INTEGRA, io-homecontrol EN PICK&CLICK! ZIJN GEREGISTREERDE HANDELSMERKEN GEBRUIKT ONDER LICENTIE DOOR DE VELUX GROEP.

kempapenberg

AROUND THE TABLE

WHAT DRIVES YOU TO WORK ABROAD?

WHAT DRIVES YOU TO WORK ABROAD?

TEXT Pieter T'Jonck

This second part of the discussion focuses on why architects wish to export their services. The reasons seem to be very diverse. Different generations also see things differently. But a desire to export is not sufficient in itself, of course. There must also be a demand. What drives foreigners to call on Belgians? What are their main qualities? They seem to cover more grounds than expected.

AUDREY CONTESSE Why in fact do you wish to work abroad?

ISIDORE ZIELONKA For a large firm like ours it's a necessity. Architecture is a cyclical profession. I have gone through four economic crises in my career. If, like Art & Build, you have 100 staff members, then you start getting pretty worried when you see another one coming. In 2006 we saw another such storm on the horizon and decided to manage at least 30% of our portfolio abroad. If the Belgian market were then to drop by 50%, you could still maintain your turnover at a level of 70%. That's well worth holding on to.

KENNETH GROOSMAN As an architectural firm, VK concentrates especially on the healthcare sector. We are more or less the market leader in Belgium in that field. But the possibilities for growth are limited, and exporting to neighbouring countries is not all that obvious since they have roughly the same skills and know-how as us, and that is the product we offer. That is why we went in search of other markets. We recently built a hospital in Vietnam, and we are now active in Russia and Kazakhstan.

CHRISTINE DE RUIJTER We have never considered export as a goal in itself. You first have to ask yourself what your qualities are. You have to be able to do what you're good at, and then the context and manner of collaborating must also suit you. Language is thus very important. That's why the Netherlands was a good opportunity for us. Maybe one day we'll get an offer to work in China, but we will only take up that offer if those conditions are met. You also have to ask yourself what is worth being exported. There have been lots of Architectural Yearbooks in Flanders in which the lion's share of projects consists of housing. That makes no sense. Working abroad is in any case a big investment. You have to aim for the long term.

ISIDORE ZIELONKA That's very true. The question is whether you position yourself as a businessman who will strike once and take the loot, or whether you work as an industrialist with a long-term perspective.

CHRISTINE DE RUIJTER We also faced the relapse of the

Dutch market. Even though it was never our intention to become a major player, we nevertheless grew into something big. And then you want to keep the team together. We thus adapted our organization so that we could fill more tasks ourselves, tasks which we would have outsourced to local offices in the past. That way you have a buffer.

FREEK PERSYN For us things are very clear: we're looking for solid, ambitious clients with challenging commissions. Were they present here, then perhaps we wouldn't go to Albania. Over the years we've noticed that there is not such a big difference between working here and abroad. The essence is the same. What changes is especially the way in which you obtain work abroad. On the other hand, a corporate culture also emerges thanks to work abroad. You don't put all your eggs in the same basket. The point is rather that we never started out from the idea of not working on the international stage.

WARD VERBAKEL I get the feeling that the younger generation sees internationalization differently. We were brought up on it. While older firms first built up a reputation locally and then made the jump abroad, we as a firm have always thought internationally because our team is also international. Another difference is that this generation operates much faster as a network of kindred spirits.

HAN VERSCHURE That's an extremely important new trend. The big firms are dinosaurs. In my view, the future belongs to networks of smaller entities in various countries that work together occasionally or structurally. The influence of university programmes like Erasmus was a decisive factor in that respect. They led to a natural formation of international groups.

WARD VERBAKEL On the other hand you have to be sure you aren't guilty of exoticism or some new kind of colonialism.

AUDREY CONTESSE What makes Belgian architects interesting for foreign clients? In what way do they stand out?

OSWALD DELLICOUR There is no Belgian architecture culture in the sense of a style or design method that can be exported. It's more about a way of approaching a project: in a professional manner, with a solid building background that goes hand in hand with an intelligent understanding of the project.

DANIEL DETHIER This is a small country, and that's a handicap since we lack a certain aura. Neither do we have a ready-made product. So you have to make choices. Belgians have a long tradition of solid professional expertise. It is not unusual here for an architect to work out minute details. That has long been, I think, the hallmark of Belgian architects. If that is what we want to export then we have to realize that we have to highlight that quality. In the past we were masters in the field of stability, but that knowledge is now available much more widely. We still excel, however, in special techniques in the field of durability and in our attention for execution techniques. I have noticed that there are now young offices like that of Julien De Smedt that throw themselves onto vast projects and also obtain them. They operate within a kind of international style. The reverse side of the coin is that behind that export, there is little thorough knowledge of building itself.

JEAN-YVES DEL FORNO The question is indeed what added value you still have to offer if, like us, you mostly work with countries with a comparable level of knowledge. The Millau Viaduct is a case in point. It was designed by Norman Foster and was initially conceived as a concrete structure. The French are also very familiar with that technology, but it turned out not to be a solution. Thanks to the research conducted at the University of Liège, we, on the other hand, have much expertise in the field of steel structures, where we are 15 years ahead of France. And with that technology it did seem possible to build the bridge at a feasible price.

DANIEL DETHIER What is remarkable is that, as in many of your constructions, your design also took into account the execution, and could therefore keep the cost down.

ARCHITECTURE IS A PHYSICAL PRODUCT, BUT IF YOU DON'T ARTICULATE ITS VALUE, THEN PEOPLE WON'T BE ABLE TO INTERPRET IT.

FREEK PERSYN

WARD VERBAKEL The professionalism you discern is perhaps due to the legal definition of the architect's mission. He has a tremendous responsibility in Belgium and is often, moreover, the project manager. That most naturally brings with it a larger sense of openness and attention for other fields of expertise in the design process. Besides that, Belgium has no solid town-planning culture, although that is now changing. That's why a Belgian architect is also a bit of a town planner. He reflects on how the context in a broad sense can be influenced positively, while foreigners generally often rather create their 'product' without paying much attention to the context. Our commission in China was a success because we had made the effort to explore the local context and customs, and drew design solutions from those observations.

CHRISTINE DE RUIJTER Our first commission in the Netherlands was on the basis of a sample project in which they recognized themselves. But now it's about other things. Our expertise comes first. That also involves the ability to work around limitations by seeing them as opportunities. Durability is a key word: to build so as not to have to start over in 15 years. But no less important is the willingness to listen. We can handle participation-oriented procedures. We set up processes which include everyone. Moreover, there is our familiarity with inner-city commissions. Listening to the context is increasingly important. In sum, it means we have successfully achieved quality at every level and not just produced a nice little design.

WARD VERBAKEL We also score well on the engineering level, thanks to the strength of our trainings. They integrate morphological research with process-oriented thinking and smoothly integrate new trends such as the search for durability. We can certainly make a difference in that respect.

DANIEL DETHIER Belgians are also more modest. We pay attention to what we say, and like a sponge soak up what we hear and see. More so than French or Parisian architects, for instance, we are also more used to dealing with non-professional clients. Parisians have a tendency to turn up, do their thing and leave. We first start a discussion and see what's possible and what the client wants from us.

JÉRÔME MATTHIEU It always strikes me that in Belgium you have to work in situations where there is no clear town-planning or legal framework or where it is, on the contrary, extremely restrictive. And yet I don't see how you can make good architecture if there is no good town planning. And yet you manage to do so. As an amateur diver I know that Belgians have the best reputation since they operate in dark underground waters where you can't see anything. It's kind of the same for Belgian architects: they have to ensure they make do in rather murky waters. (Laughter all around)

CHRISTINE DE RUIJTER I don't think we can still talk in such negative terms about Belgium, or at least about Flanders. Twenty years ago that was certainly the case, and for us it was a breath of fresh air to work in the Netherlands. We now notice, by contrast, that we can apply here the experience we gathered there. We are now importing what we first exported.

WARD VERBAKEL I agree. During a recent training for burgomasters at Columbia University in New York, Antwerp's town-planning policy was mentioned as an exemplary practice. I also notice that foreigners are interested in what can be seen here: our sensitivity in designing suburbs, for instance.

FREEK PERSYN It is an interesting thought that export can change your own culture. A country sends out its sons in order to bring them back. The question is whether you could work on that more deliberately. That's not the case at present. It's just an observation.

PIETER T'JONCK Do we even have anything to offer less-developed countries? So far we have especially been discussing large projects built according to our standards.

OSWALD DELLICOUR It is paradoxical, but I think that

we can offer added value in developing countries given that we know their situation better. A professional class has emerged since the 1960s that was trained here. They strongly identify with our globalized building style, while we, on the other hand, given our colonial past and professional expertise, are more focused on the value of local building methods and a local culture. There is no point in using a glass façade in the tropics because the cooling load is unacceptably high. We would then suggest using earth. What's more, local labourers know that technique a lot better.

PIETER T'JONCK Freek Persyn, for the tower in Tirana you also made use of local opportunities, I believe?

FREEK PERSYN When designing the project we already tried to imagine what would be locally possible and appropriate. On site we realized that none of it worked. We explored what margin of error you had to take into consideration. The local engineer saw it as a victory that he had done better than usual, but we saw that his precision was nevertheless merely relative. They are well-trained professionals, but they don't have the competence of a firm like Bureau Greisch. It's just as Oswald Dellicour already said: you have to have the ambition to do it better than what you can do today, but not necessarily incredibly better. Doing something 'Western' makes no sense. We didn't go to Tirana to tell them how to do things, but to discover what was suitable. As an outsider you can see that better.

HAN VERSCHURE That is a significant development. We are here talking about the export of knowledge, but in my opinion the next 30 years will increasingly involve a reciprocal learning process. We do have a bit of a technological head start, but our attention for a careful management of the environment has traditionally never been that great. Just look at the problems we have with flooding. Real culture consists in discovering in other cultures what they can teach us. This also involves issues like town planning: learning from the manner in which people elsewhere give shape to their society.

BELGIANS HAVE A LONG TRADITION OF SOLID PROFESSIONAL EXPERTISE.

DANIEL DETHIER

styles in carpet tiles

CONVERSE

CONNEXXION   COLOR&   METALLIC

We inspire, you create, we develop

modulyss® creates, produces and sells carpet tiles, and is geared to architects who are looking for high-quality and trendy carpet tiles. modulyss® carpet tiles are available in different colours, structures and patterns. The creative possibilities are endless. The products can be used independently but also in combination with each other to give the floor an added dimension and an exclusive look. modulyss® is a partner that thinks and acts proactively from the conception stage to the execution.

More information: modulyss® | T +32 (0)52 45 72 11 | info@modulyss.com | www.modulyss.com

AROUND THE TABLE

HOW DO YOU START EXPORTING?

HOW DO YOU START EXPORTING?

TEXT Pieter T'Jonck

It emerged earlier that, although a certain dynamic has already been put in place, the various Belgian authorities contribute little to the export of architecture – at least for now – compared to the neighbouring countries. The Dutch and the French even make good use of the cultural circuit. From the following discussion, it seems that the cultural circuit also yields other advantages. Whether they grew out of the civil service or the Erasmus programme, older and more recent networks also seem to be important leverage tools to be able to work abroad, whether as regards invitations for competitions or commissions that were granted directly. Good relations with property developers also often seem to pay off. Clients, however, increasingly ask for a complete package, whereby architects are merely a cog in the wheel of international consultancies. Is growth therefore a necessity, or are there other possibilities? Do Belgian firms have to join forces so that their specific skills complement one another? Which authority can ensure that the right partners find one another? The conversation ultimately focused on the question as to how to get insight into the local situation, and how one organizes the work there in practice. What is the role of the local partner, whether a client or local architectural firm? How does one deal with (at times very big) differences in (building) culture, expectations as regards the architect, and fees?

PIETER T'JONCK How does one develop a name for oneself abroad?

PRUDENT DE WISPELAERE For us things began both in the Netherlands and in France with an exhibition that was well prepared and heavily publicized. The impact of such an event can be felt for years. Even after 15 years there were people in the Netherlands who said they knew us through the Berlage Fair exhibition.

FREEK PERSYN As Belgians we have a problem in this respect. Here only architects take part in exhibitions. Clients, building contractors, developers are nowhere to be seen there. The 'cultural' sector (Bozar, de Singel, etc.) and 'commercial' architecture (MIPIM, etc.) are separate circuits in this country.

OSWALD DELLICOUR The reason is an obvious lack of cultural awareness among clients, and the root of that problem is to be found in education. Only if an architectural culture is passed on will you get clients who can manage their task fully, who know how to choose an architect.

AURORE BORACZEK On the French-speaking side, the CIVA (International Centre for the City, Architecture and Landscape) has organized good exhibitions which we also wish to have travel internationally. We want to build up a discourse around these exhibitions with workshops and encounters.

AUDREY CONTESSE How much clout does a firm need to export its services with any measure of success?

PRUDENT DE WISPELAERE Size is not intrinsically a problem, although a problem has emerged in recent years due to a change in mentality among clients. We deliberately chose to remain small at the time. Our firm only totals some eight staff members. It is hard to imagine that we could still be considered for a job like the university hospital of Sart-Tilman, and yet we were. The profession has become a lot more complex, however. Furthermore, clients no longer want to work with different parties, such as an engineer, an architect, etc. They want one contact person and therefore choose major players like

Arcadis. The architect then becomes a subcontractor. You thus lose that direct contact with the client. That's certainly not to the advantage of the design.

HAN VERSCHURE And yet those large organizations don't offer much quality. Construction might move along smoothly, but they stick to tested methods. That doesn't necessarily deliver a lasting result nor a high degree of architectural quality or at the level of town planning. As I said before: in my opinion, those large firms are going to die out in the long run.

JÉRÔME MATTHIEU I also disagree. We are always looking to work with architects, not with organizations. It is first and foremost an 'intuitu personae' business, one that relies on the personality of the other party.

ISIDORE ZIELONKA But surely you can't ignore the fact that you're hardly visible on the international stage beneath a certain size. In Belgium you matter if you have 25 staff workers, in Europe if you have at least 250, and on the world stage 500 is the norm. That means that in Belgium we are forced to work together if we wish to take on large French or English firms – especially in matters of competitions and selections. Beneath a certain size you simply don't count.

WARD VERBAKEL That's changing. For some commissions you do indeed have to prove that you have already built 520 hospitals, but in more and more selections, the choice is made based purely on the portfolio. That way you can show what you're worth based on theoretical projects or town-planning studies.

ISIDORE ZIELONKA That remains marginal, no more than 10% of cases. There is a tendency to ask a young office to be part of a team that is applying. We do that more and more often. One can imagine a database that for that purpose would inventorize the specific competences of firms. One should even imagine that in a European perspective. The economic importance thereof is enormous. We really shouldn't think that we are still going to be assembling cars here in the future. We will have to make do with this production of knowledge.

DANIEL DETHIER Then we have to stop forcing competitions into a straitjacket of references. That blocks everything. I even fear that architects themselves are guilty of this state of affairs because they want to share the market. Besides, that doesn't hold only for the international market. In Belgium, too, that messes up everything.

FREEK PERSYN I notice, however, that we, as a 'small' firm, are often called on, like now for the redevelopment of Bordeaux. And yet they know that we don't have much expertise and they sometimes make that very clear. What interests them is that we don't have any preconceived ideas, but ask ourselves what the meaning of things is. That can't be described rationally. And yet it is a specific competence: choosing a position that helps things move forward.

PIETER T'JONCK If we hold on to Isidore Zielonka's thought for a minute: who could provide such a database?

JÉRÔME MATTHIEU That should be a task for the Order of Architects. As a former lawyer I know that the Order of Lawyers has done excellent work at that level in recent years. From a merely repressive authority it has grown into an organization that also promotes the profession… (All other participants express their strong disagreement)

CHRISTINE DE RUIJTER We've rarely received any support from the order, but plenty of opposition. When they realized that we were very active in the Netherlands, they only wanted to recognize internships in our office for six months because it involved 'specialized internships abroad'. The contrast with the BNA (the Royal Institute of Dutch architects), of which we have in the meantime become members, is pitiful. They have given us real support in a lot of areas.

PIETER T'JONCK Is this not a job for the academic world?

OSWALD DELLICOUR That's certainly the case in the US. I remember that the message we received when I graduated was: 'You're not leaving us, we're leaving with you'. We're a far way away from that in Belgium.

HOW DO YOU START EXPORTING?

ISIDORE ZIELONKA That corresponds to the economic reality. Such a system could give young people access to an international circuit without them first having to fight for their place on the local market.

AUDREY CONTESSE Suppose you have cleared all the hurdles and are at work abroad. How do you connect to the local context and sensitivities?

ISIDORE ZIELONKA If you work for a developer, gushing about the local context is mere hypocrisy. The developer wants to raise the same building he has already built in Brussels or in Berlin. If, on the other hand, you deal with the end-user directly or thanks to a competition, you can soak up a lot about the context from the client.

JÉRÔME MATTHIEU That's true. In Warsaw at present there is a lot of building activity but if you take a closer look you'll notice that the whole market is in the hands of German funds or insurance companies – the same ones, for that matter, which dominated the market here ten years ago… And the buildings constructed for them in Warsaw perfectly match their 'style' of product.

CHRISTINE DE RUIJTER If a foreign client wishes to make the effort to look for an architect beyond his borders, that's already a sign that he cherishes great ambitions. As a result, he'll put a lot of energy into informing the architect. Perhaps an Amsterdamer would also benefit a lot from that information if he was working in Nijmegen, but that is in fact rarely the case. It thus all seems 'self-evident', but it never is. In such an international relation you start out by definition from an attitude of mutual respect.

ISIDORE ZIELONKA What's important is that you not only connect with the local culture in the broad sense of the term, but also to the local way of working, on site, in the administration, etc. Even in a country like France the customs and sensibilities can be very different from one region to the next. Paris is neither Strasbourg nor Toulouse. There are enormous differences.

PIETER T'JONCK Is it necessary to be able to rely on a local partner?

JEAN-YVES DEL FORNO That hardly plays a role for us. We can reasonably manage our affairs from our home base.

KENNETH GROOSMAN For us it depends on the country where we are working. In Vietnam we worked with a local firm. It first went very well, later less so, and ultimately we parted ways. In Russia we are working with a small local office. In Kazakhstan we took over an office. We've noticed that it's not always easy to guarantee the quality if you don't follow up the execution yourself.

CHRISTINE DE RUIJTER We work very regularly with local offices, but you can't expect it all to be good. It doesn't free you from the obligation to immerse yourself thoroughly in the affairs, at all levels, whether cultural-historic or administrative-technical. That is also how you deliver added value. The Dutch are often left wondering at everything we get done in the field of fire safety, but that's because we've read the regulations from A to Z, and not just the headings and then checked our findings with the fire department. That's how we discover possibilities that were overlooked on location.

ISIDORE ZIELONKA It is indeed unreasonable to shift the entire execution to a local partner. Besides, you have to involve the latter in the design process. We use the following rule: during the design process we do 80% of the work and they do 20%, but the reverse during the execution. Choosing a partner is difficult, however. If you choose a small partner, then they might grow to become a rival. Either way, collaboration is difficult among architects, and not only because they have big egos. During each commission you are looking for the next commission to bring in. If two firms are working on the same project then the question is who is the 'author' of the project, because they will reap the honour and thus probably also the next commission.

JÉRÔME MATTHIEU We often work in combination with a Belgian and a local firm. For us, two principles have to be guaranteed: the execution must correspond to predefined 'Belgian' standards, and the administrative

AS A SMALL COUNTRY, OUR ATTENTION HAS, HISTORICALLY, ALWAYS BEEN TURNED OUTWARDS.

OSWALD DELLICOUR

transactions have to go smoothly. In Warsaw we would certainly have solved this by coupling Belgian and Polish architects together: the latter know the local situation, the former have the know-how.

OSWALD DELLICOUR We haven't yet evoked the issue of fees here, but in collaborations with developing countries, it's not an easy thing. Our custom is to work out the details of the buildings, but with the fees that are applicable there it's just not feasible. An architect there often delivers little more than a little sketch with some measures. Other building partners will then take care of the execution. A German firm recently won the competition for the Central Bank of Turkey, for instance, but the deal fell through because no agreement could be found on the fees.

DANIEL DETHIER The level of technical know-how required in those countries is also much lower. You don't have to deal with the annoying cold bridges, but you do have to deal with questions of air conditioning… I think, however, that there are opportunities there. It is worth developing a project together with a good building contractor.

ISIDORE ZIELONKA The exchange rates are playing tricks on us in this respect. At present it is virtually impossible to compete with US firms, because their dollar is worth just as much to them as our euro, but once converted, that makes us roughly 30% more expensive.

The discussion is far from over. This very transcript represents only a fraction of the many considerations and insights expressed by participants during the discussion. What is clear is that exporting architecture is no univocal or simple matter, and that its execution can meet with many problems. On the other hand, export also seems to offer many growth opportunities for Belgian firms and to provide strong cultural stimuli. This is a story to be continued.

A dynamic and experienced partner at your side.

Bulex®

Always at your side

Bulex Heat Pumps

The Genia AIR is the new Heat Pump series in the Bulex range, with outputs from 8,12 and 15kW. Its innovative technology and its capacity to work alone or combined with a Bulex boiler or any other heating source make the Genia AIR the right solution for any heating system.

Efficient solutions.
Heating. Hot water.

WWW.WBARCHITECTURES.BE

WALLONIE-BRUXELLES ARCHITECTURES

THE INTERNATIONAL PROMOTION OF ARCHITECTS FROM THE WALLONIA-BRUSSELS FEDERATION

———

WBA IS A SUPPORT AGENCY DEDICATED
TO THE DEVELOPMENT AND RECOGNITION
OF ARCHITECTS AND RELATED PROFESSIONS
(SUCH AS TOWN PLANNERS AND LANDSCAPERS)
ON THE INTERNATIONAL SCENE.

———

Contact
contact@wbarchitectures.be

Wallonie-Bruxelles Architectures
Place Sainctelette, 2, 1080 Brussels

P +32 2 421 83 64
F +32 2 421 83 69

BELGIAN ARCHITECTS ARE ESPECIALLY PRACTICE-ORIENTED ARCHITECTS.

Hart Tilman

Belgian, or Flemish architecture at least, has undoubtedly undergone a radical transformation over the past 20 years. Thanks to such initiatives as the Flanders Spatial Structure Plan, the Architectural Yearbooks, the Flemish Government Architect, and the Open Call, a climate has gradually been created in which a greater sense of responsibility, improved professionalism and increased transparency are contributing to an architectural environment of higher standards. What is no less remarkable in this regard is the fact that the style of the architecture has progressively become more radical but also more homogenized: neo-modernist minimalism is increasingly dominant. Old-fashioned qualities such as improvisation and expressivity are more and more rare, which is sometimes regrettable. After encountering the umpteenth neatly detailed abstract box while leafing through one or other yearbook, one longs for something lively, something unfamiliar and surprising.

Fortunately this longing is increasingly being heard, also within Belgian architecture. Five years ago, in response to the ubiquitous minimalism, Willem Jan Neutelings proclaimed 'maximalism', which would bring about the end of 'good taste'. The recent frenzy surrounding the opening of Museum Aan de Stroom (MAS) in Antwerp, designed by Neutelings Riedijk Architects, seems to prove that a change is in the making.

Arthur Wortmann
Editor in chief | Mark

MASSIMILISM

BELGIAN ARCHITECTURE BEYOND BELGIUM?

From a German perspective, I first like to recall Henry van de Velde, who was active in Germany between 1900 and 1930 and who, in light of Belgian art nouveau, represented a great enrichment for the country. Particularly noteworthy are his School of Arts and Crafts in Weimar, and the villas in Chemnitz, Hagen and Gera.

There are, in my view, currently three firms in particular that have drawn attention in Europe and gained a certain foothold there. Xaveer De Geyter is present on the international architecture and town-planning scene, and has taken part in major competitions in the Netherlands, France and Switzerland. His Chasse Park Apartments in Breda are disputed, but have also received much praise. Robbrecht en Daem Architecten is the second firm I wish to mention, since they have blazed a very specific and interesting trail, and already enjoy a solid reputation abroad. However, they have no significant commissions outside Belgium, and only the municipal archives building in Bordeaux is in the planning stages. Last but not least, Stéphane Beel is also worth highlighting. The elegance and clarity of his designs have established his reputation outside Belgium. He has so far completed housing projects in Lille and Boulogne-Billancourt.

An idiosyncratic Belgian signature is not discernible, and even the renowned firms, I believe, tend to follow international trends in an increasingly interconnected world. There is one exception, however, which seems important to me, and that is the tremendous creativity, but also the certain singularity, to be found in the architecture of Belgian family homes, or in the conversions of those typical small single-family houses, often detached, found in generally modest areas. Regardless of whether in the north or the south of the country, this architecture, with all its idiosyncrasies, always meets with surprise abroad.

Sebastian Redecke
Editor in chief | Bauwelt

Once one does away with local factors – climatic, regulatory or economic constraints – can one still talk of regional or national architectures in 2012? Architectural training in Europe has now been harmonized. Architects travel, study (thanks to the Erasmus programme) and do internships outside their homeland. The references given in architectural reviews are now international. Regulations in terms of safety, accessibility and the environment are becoming standardized. So what is there to say, from a Parisian perspective, on architecture in Belgium? Perhaps that creativity there seems less flashy than in France, that the work on light seems to rely less on a geometric approach, seems less influenced by Le Corbusier. Or that light is seen less as a luminous flux that is to be mastered and more as a presence, a densification of space. And just as I thought I could safely say that there is no Belgian specificity, I recall the beautiful house designed by Pierre Hebbelinck in Brussels, its light-absorbing volumes, its magnificent brickwork with overflowing joints: why, this must be Belgium!

Emmanuel Caille
Editor in chief | d'A

BELGIAN?

THE BELGIAN PAVILION IN THE GIARDINI HAS REGULARLY BEEN NUMBERED AMONG THE POSITIVE SURPRISES OF THE VENICE ARCHI-TECTURE BIENNALE.

Caspar Schärer

OFFICE KGDVS | BAS PRINCEN

TEXT Cécile Vandernoot
PHOTOGRAPHY Bas Princen

In the 'Garden Pavilion' at the end of the Arsenale, the architects of Office KGDVS found a way to depict what fascinates them in a moderate space, thanks to and through an ongoing visual search. A dialogue runs through the '7 rooms and 21 perspectives'. The spatialization of the representational collages of projects and of the photographic work of Bas Princen reveals, on the other hand, much more than concerns. "We have reached the pinnacle of a collaboration. The works cohabit tangibly in the pavilion while the entire set remains at the dream stage of what an architectural vision represents", explains David Van Severen. The light cotton canopy and its aerial structural columns prolong the pavilion and generate a 'reception' space at the end of the Biennale. This specific, drawn space meets an untamed nature that has been shaped to become a readable space, a meeting point for visitors. This very sober intervention is also minimal due to the nature of things: building on the Lagoon and transporting materials there were the major constraints (the architects had experienced this two years earlier with 'After the Party').

The Golden Lion that they were awarded in 2010 brought them a lot of attention from that cultural sphere as well as some nice opportunities, although the latter did not always result in tangible projects, however. This left the office the time to develop at its own pace. "Whether we are local or international architects is of no real importance. The realization of a project in a cultural context makes us international for our architectural discourse is so in itself. The idea of export exists through the visibility of a project, whether it gets built in Brussels, Flanders, Chile, or elsewhere", says Kersten Geers. Architectural discourse travels, disseminates and exports itself, and is maintained through intellectual exchanges with an international stage in the broad sense. "Building abroad is quite recent for our office. So far our interventions have been temporary, which doesn't make for an easier process, but simply a different one. The current projects that are taking shape abroad find their origin in invitations from other architects. This network and the local partners are important in order to adopt a coherent professional conduct", concludes Kersten Geers.

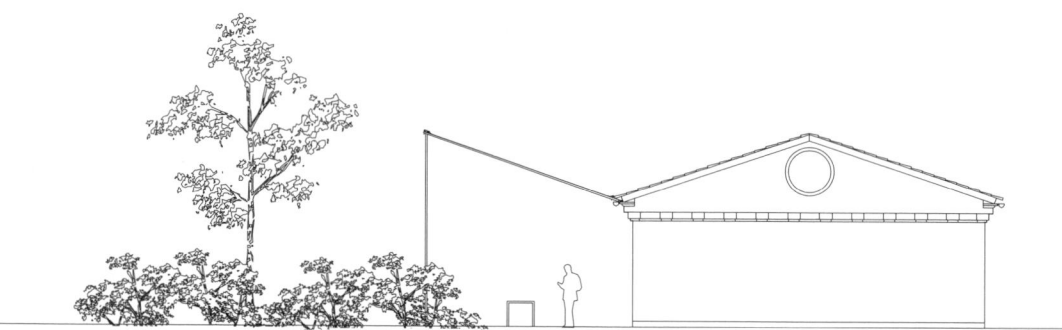

Office Kersten Geers David Van Severen sheds some light on what it means to win the Silver Lion at the Venice Architecture Biennale.

THE LIGHT COTTON CANOPY AND ITS AERIAL
STRUCTURAL COLUMNS PROLONG THE
PAVILION AND GENERATE A 'RECEPTION' SPACE
AT THE END OF THE BIENNALE.

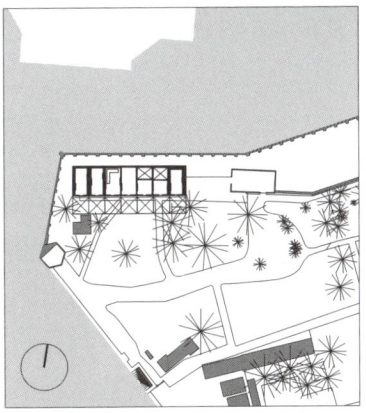

Garden Pavilion (7 Rooms / 21 Perspectives)

PROGRAMME pavilion
PROCEDURE invitation
ARCHITECT Office KGDVS + Bas Princen
CLIENT La Biennale di Venezia
STABILITY UTIL
BUDGET (excluding VAT and fees) 15 000 euro
COMPLETED August 2010
www.officekgdvs.com

GULELE BOTANIC GARDEN
ADDIS ABABA | ETHIOPIA
SYNERGY INTERNATIONAL | ABBA ARCHITECTS

TEXT Cécile Vandernoot
PHOTOGRAPHY Synergy International

Located on the outskirts of Addis Ababa in Ethiopia, a large green area of 740 hectares offers considerable development opportunities. "The city is experiencing a strong demographic expansion: it currently comprises 8 million inhabitants", explains Oswald Dellicour, an associate architect with the architectural firm Synergy International. "In order to plan and preserve this area, we were called on to prepare – briefly – a master plan". Co-authored with the Belgian landscape architecture firm JNC International, this report led to a reflection on the interaction between city, country and nature, while the outskirts of the park that has been earmarked to become a botanical garden were sketched out schematically. An international architecture competition was then launched.

Temporarily associated with the local firm Abba Architects, Synergy International and JNC won the competition in 2008. They proposed a series of essential measures for the conservation of the site's ecosystem and biosphere, and the introduction of several educational tools to raise the population's awareness on environmental issues.

Thus, the gradual felling of a forest of eucalyptus trees imported from Australia and that was present on the site will contribute to the redevelopment of native vegetation. The felled eucalyptuses will then serve as raw material for the construction of the buildings: particles from their trunks will be mixed with clay to form bricks of sun-dried earth, called 'adobes'. The felled trunks will in part be cut up into strips (3 x 10 x 120 cm) and assembled in glued laminated timber (a first in Ethiopia) to be used for the primary span and into other logs to be used as frames for the secondary span of the large undulating roofs, an architectural design inspired by the shape of eucalyptus leaves. The rest of the materials that will make up the shell, such as the natural stones used for the foundation, will come almost exclusively from the immediate surroundings. These techniques, combining ancestral resources and expertise, have sometimes been forgotten or find their source in other African countries. "While the transmission of the techniques we master is not commercially interesting, it is undeniably worthwhile in terms of development. The idea is to rely on local materials essentially and to use techniques that generate a lot of jobs".

In terms of architecture, however, the search for the 'right gesture' is less obvious in a context where the building culture is quite different from the one in Belgium. Indeed, there are many different understandings of the notion of 'the art of building'. The idea of transmission has to be kept in mind, and "the near daily monitoring of the site is essential". This, in turn, was sometimes a source of problems as regards the payment of services when fees are calculated based on local construction costs.

While the cost of the Gulele Botanic Garden is a third of what it would be in Europe, the project managers have made the effort to respect the scale fee system of the Royal Institute of British Architects (RIBA) to determine the architects' fees. This has made it possible to ensure the necessary technical assistance during construction, which would otherwise not always be the case.

In Belgium, too, we seek the same "right gesture" in terms of energy and building methods while continuing to conduct the projects in an effective manner.

"One of the firm's dreams would be to deduct a percentage from Belgian projects, which would then be reinvested in projects on the other side of the world, where making ends meet is not easy".

Whether immersed in the development of African countries or in details of contemporary architecture in Belgium, Synergy International always takes the same ecological approach, a sign of the high level of coherence it seeks.

GULELE BOTANIC GARDEN
ADDIS ABABA | ETHIOPIA
SYNERGY INTERNATIONAL | ABBA ARCHITECTS

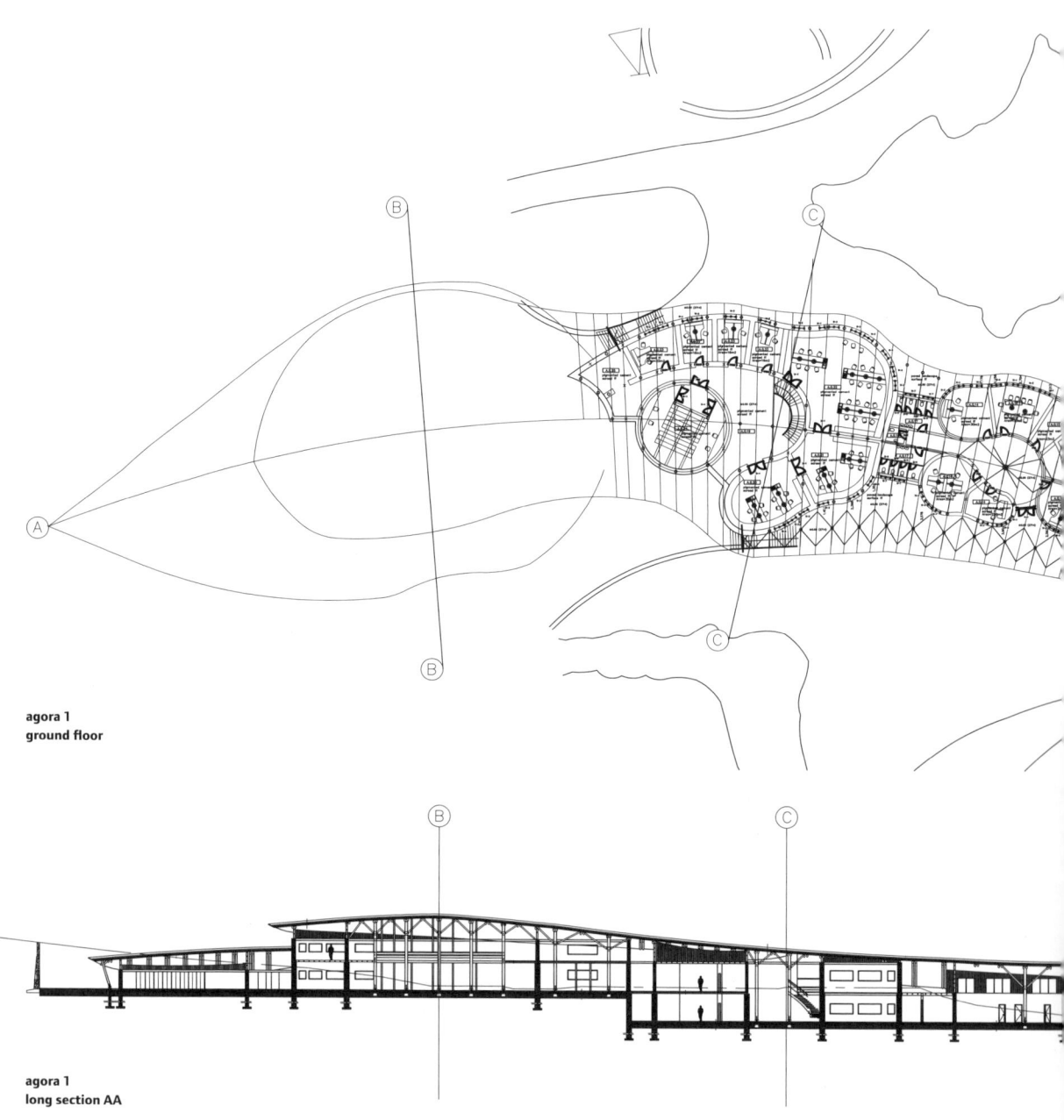

agora 1
ground floor

agora 1
long section AA

ONE OF THE FIRM'S DREAMS IS TO DEDUCT A
PERCENTAGE FROM BELGIAN PROJECTS, WHICH
WOULD THEN BE REINVESTED IN PROJECTS
ON THE OTHER SIDE OF THE WORLD, WHERE
MAKING ENDS MEET IS NOT EASY.

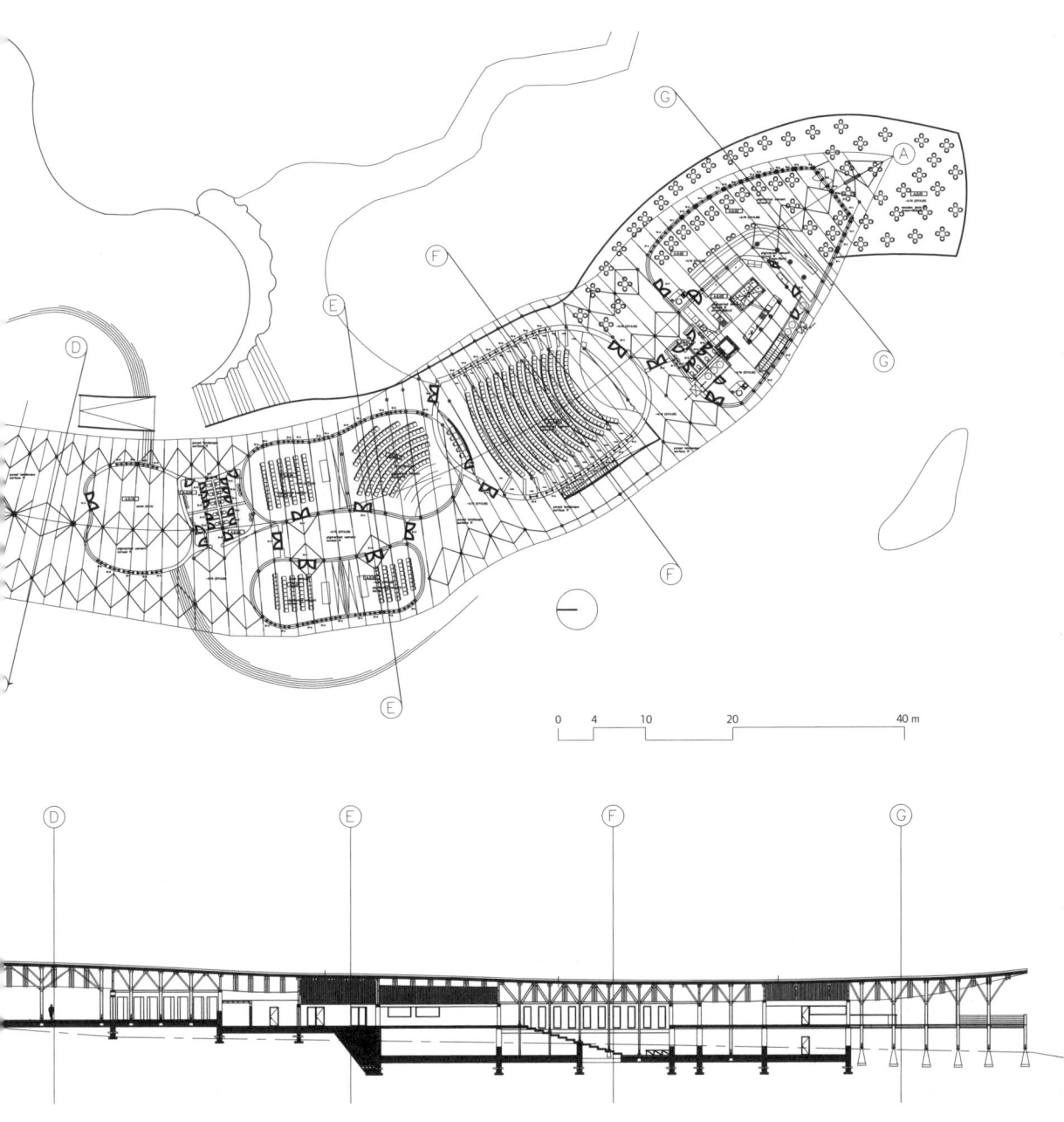

GULELE BOTANIC GARDEN
ADDIS ABABA | ETHIOPIA
SYNERGY INTERNATIONAL | ABBA ARCHITECTS

Gulele botanic garden

PROGRAMME lay-out of a park located on the outskirts of Addis Ababa and covering a naturally protected area, botanical garden, regional centre for the environment, seed bank, herbarium, and educational equipment open to the public PROCEDURE international competition
ARCHITECT Synergy International | Abba Architects
CLIENT the city of Addis Ababa and the faculty of science of the university of Addis Ababa
LANDSCAPE ARCHITECT JNC International
STABILITY | TECHNIQUES Syneff Consult
STRUCTURAL WORK | CARPENTRY | FAÇADE | ELECTRICITY | HEATING | WORKMANSHIP OF INTERIOR Flintstone Contractors
AREA building 8 000 m² | botanical garden 500 000 m² | park in total 7 000 000 m²
BUDGET (excluding VAT and fees) 17 000 000 euro
COMPLETED May 2012
www.synergy-international.com

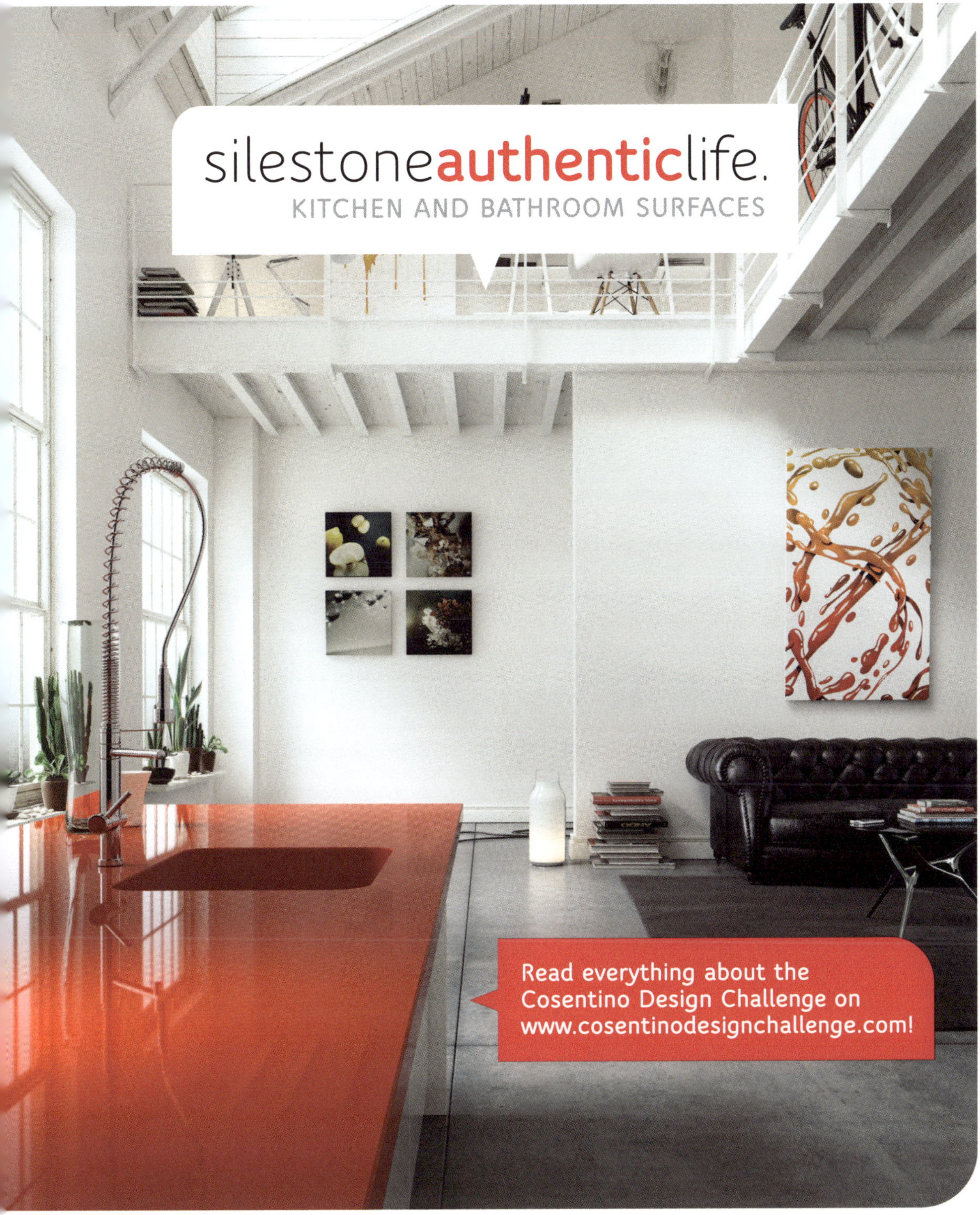

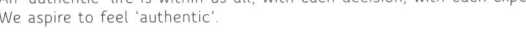

CHARLES VANDENHOVE ET ASSOCIÉS

TEXT Gilles Béchet
PHOTOGRAPHY Philippe Vander Maren

For some 20 years already, the Liège-based architect Charles Vandenhove has built almost exclusively in the Netherlands. "It is a country that is open to innovation and to foreign architects. Our first contract, a housing project in The Hague, came in response to a request made by a residents' committee that had been won over by what we had done in the neighbourhood of Hors-Château and the Rue des Brasseurs in Liège. This project then led to another one, and so on", says the architect Prudent Dewispelaere. In 2004, the municipality of Ridderkerk, a town located south of Rotterdam, commissioned Charles Vandenhove to design a mixed building that would house both the town hall and various cultural services. Only six firms were invited to take part in the competition. The sketch he proposed – combining classic architectural grammar, functional and spacious volumes, and significant artistic interventions – stood out. The project, which included both the renovation of the former town hall and the creation of new spaces distributed around a large hall, also involved designing the furniture and fittings as well as the completion of all public spaces: a comprehensive project, therefore, and one that is not only very gratifying, but also increasingly rare for architects. The municipality commissioned an engineering consultancy to supervise the coordination among all parties involved in the project. But for Charles Vandenhove, it was essential to be able to work on an equal footing with all contracting parties, with no supervision other than from the project manager. "We insisted on having that direct line. It is a matter of independence and liberty. There can be no quality architecture without mutual trust and the support of a project manager who can lend his vision to the project. This is what makes it possible for us to create a world which, users of the building will realize, is the result of the intervention of an architect, and not mere underlings".

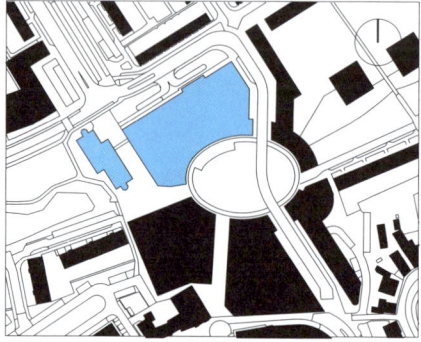

Ridderkerk community and multifunctional centre

PROGRAMME community and multifunctional centre
PROCEDURE competition by invitation
ARCHITECT Charles Vandenhove et Associés, Architectes
CLIENT the city of Ridderkerk STABILITY Van der Vorm
TECHNIQUES | EPB Arcadis ACOUSTICS Peutz Bouwfysica
STRUCTURAL WORK | FAÇADE| WORKMANSHIP OF INTERIOR
Visser & Smit Bouw CARPENTRY Alcoa
ELECTRICITY | HEATING Nomij AREA 15 500 m²
BUDGET (excluding VAT and fees) 20 000 000 euro
COMPLETED January 2005
www.charlesvandenhove.be

The new town hall of Ridderkerk, in the Netherlands, is the work of Charles Vandenhove. The architect ensured he would work directly with the project manager on this comprehensive building project.

RIDDERKERK COMMUNITY AND MULTIFUNCTIONAL CENTRE
RIDDERKERK | NETHERLANDS
CHARLES VANDENHOVE ET ASSOCIÉS

THERE CAN BE NO QUALITY ARCHITECTURE
WITHOUT MUTUAL TRUST AND THE SUPPORT
OF A PROJECT MANAGER WHO CAN LEND HIS
VISION TO THE PROJECT.

RIDDERKERK COMMUNITY AND MULTIFUNCTIONAL CENTRE
RIDDERKERK | NETHERLANDS
CHARLES VANDENHOVE ET ASSOCIÉS

long section

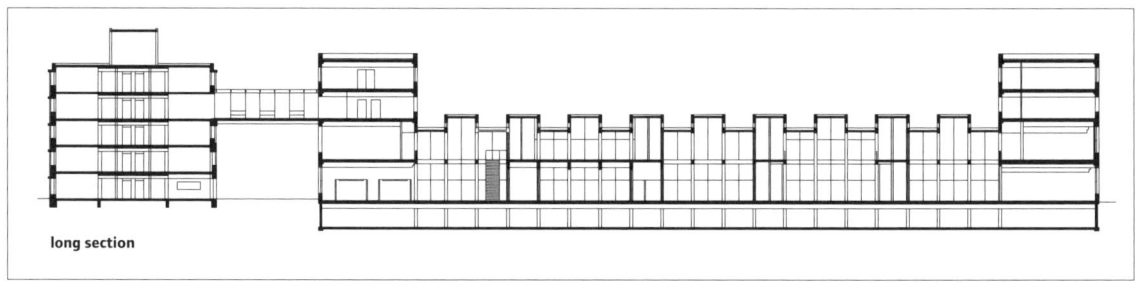

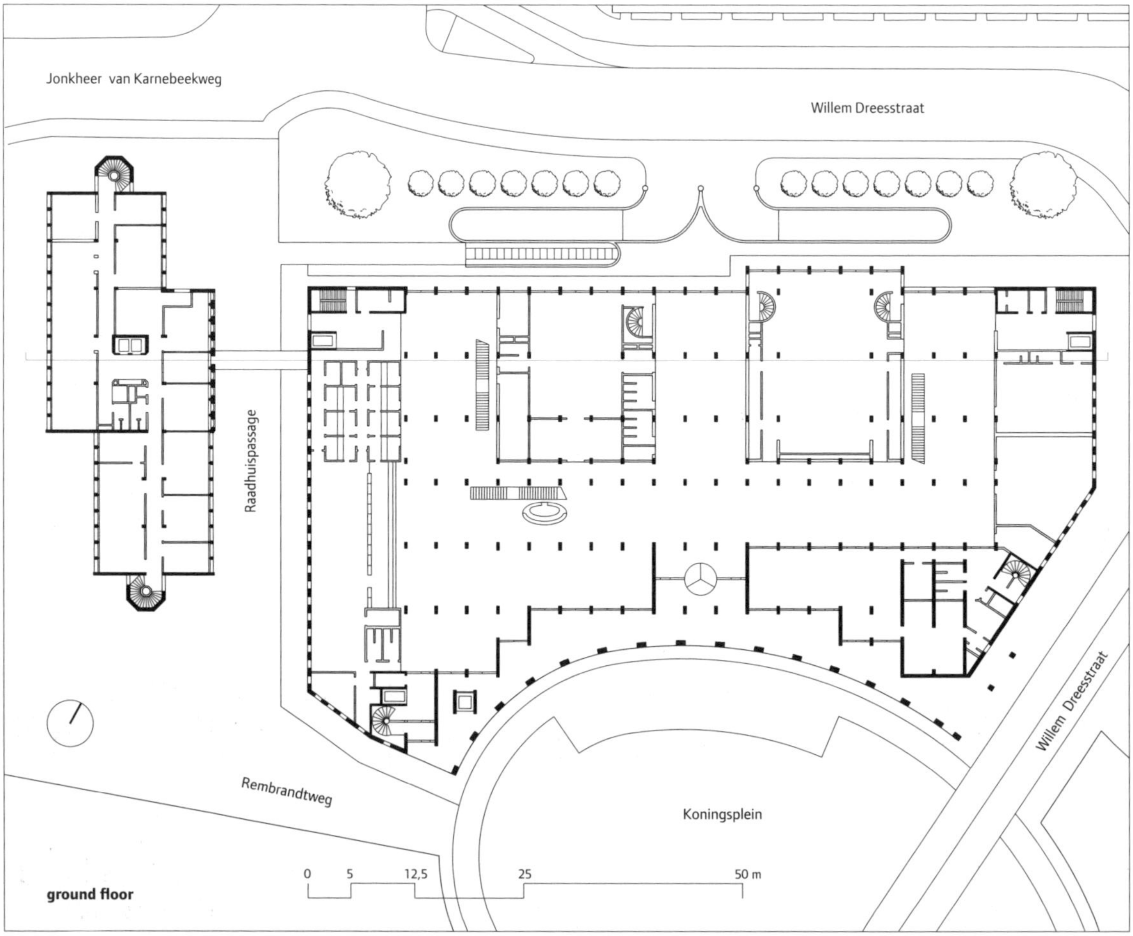

Jonkheer van Karnebeekweg

Willem Dreesstraat

Raadhuispassage

Rembrandtweg

Koningsplein

Willem Dreesstraat

0   5   12,5   25   50 m

ground floor

BODART & GONAY

PHENIX 120 GREEN

Imagine an universe which resembles to you,
a space of comfort and wellbeing where the softness of the flame
accompanies you in the best moments of your life.

Phenix green, the ecological* fireplace with a retraclable door by BG !

a part of you

* The Phenix 120 green of BG rejects less
than 0.09% of CO in the atmosphere.

BRUNO ALBERT | JO COENEN | SNELDER VOLA PETIT

TEXT Gilles Béchet

"Public-private partnerships are not all that common, yet they constitute the ideal mix needed to transform a city", says Bruno Albert, one of the two architects chosen to realize the Mosae Forum in Maastricht. It is through an international competition that the Liège-based architect was called on for this vast project conceived by the Maastricht-based group 3W and the local authorities for the redevelopment of an inner-city neighbourhood. The objective was to gather administrative and commercial services in a complex including offices, shops and housing units around a new square built above an underground car park. Given the scale of the project, the work was divided between two architects: Bruno Albert took charge of the southern sector, while Joe Coenen, the author of the master plan, took charge of the northern sector. "I asked that we each focus on a sector because we had already had the opportunity to work together and it had involved complex management issues". Launched in 1994, the works ended in 2008, a relatively long period due to the complexity involved in transforming the urban fabric, including its share of expropriations and demolitions. "One of the project's symbolic actions was the opening of a passageway through the ground floor of a listed townhouse to channel the flow of pedestrians between the commercial thoroughfare and the new square. Talks with heritage officials lasted almost as long as every-thing else", says the architect with a smile. Throughout the project, Bruno Albert relied on a small number of collaborators. "We were never more than ten members of staff. Many people don't understand how we managed to achieve so much with a small team. But it is thanks to this that we were able to stay on course when commissions were scarce".

The Mosae Forum was not the first collaboration between Joe Coenen and Bruno Albert. It all started with an exhibition devoted to Albert's work at the Sint Lucas school of architecture in Brussels in 1985. The exhibition was later shown in Amsterdam, where it was introduced by Coenen. This resulted in a first invitation to create 300 housing units in the port district of the Dutch capital, followed by many other projects. "Although we have taken part in several competitions, most of our projects in the Netherlands have been commissions. I believe it's all a matter of people, of personal contact and vision", says the architect with a smile.

© JEAN-LUC DERU

With the Mosae Forum in Maastricht, Bruno Albert was one of the two architects chosen to carry out an ambitious urban renovation programme. This long-term project taught the Liège-based architect to adapt to the rhythm of change in one of the city's neighbourhoods.

© JEAN-LUC DERU

MOSAE FORUM
MAASTRICHT | NETHERLANDS
BRUNO ALBERT | JO COENEN | SNELDER VOLA PETIT

© PETRA APPELHOF

© PETRA APPELHOF

© PETRA APPELHOF

THE OPENING OF A PASSAGEWAY THROUGH
THE GROUND FLOOR OF A LISTED TOWNHOUSE
TO CHANNEL THE FLOW OF PEDESTRIANS WAS
A SYMBOLIC ACTION.

© JEAN-LUC DERU

© OLIVIER WALLERAND

MOSAE FORUM
MAASTRICHT | NETHERLANDS
BRUNO ALBERT | JO COENEN | SNELDER VOLA PETIT

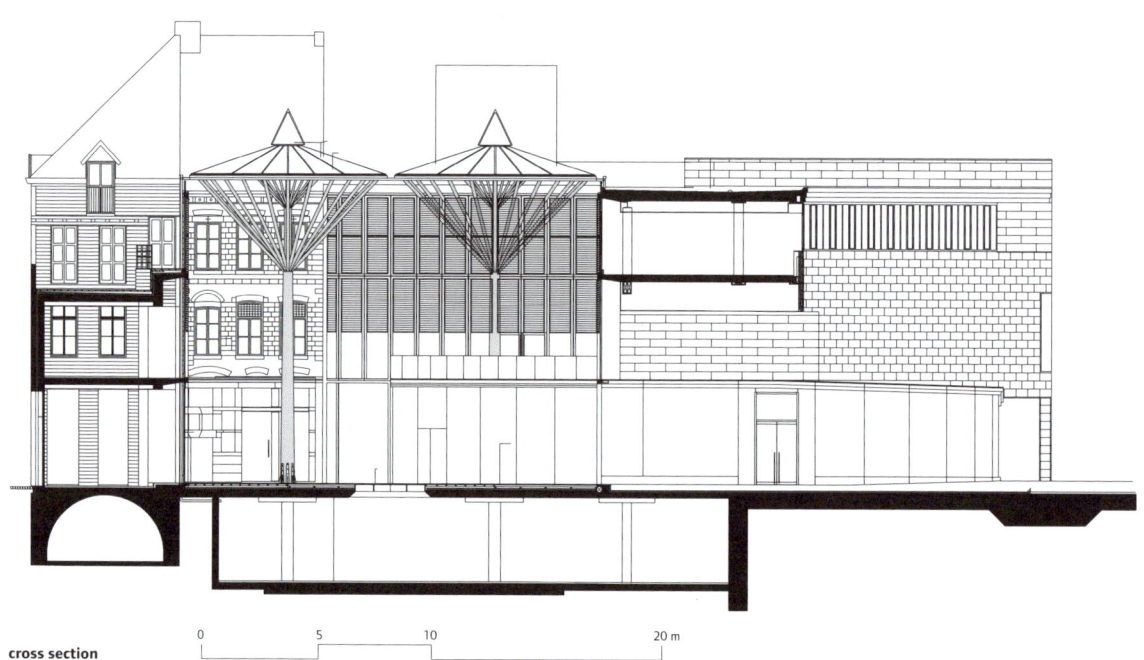

cross section

0   5   10   20 m

ground floor

0   10   20   40 m

ECONOMIC ACTIVITY

THE OBJECTIVE WAS TO GATHER
ADMINISTRATIVE AND COMMERCIAL SERVICES
IN A COMPLEX INCLUDING OFFICES, SHOPS AND
HOUSING UNITS AROUND A NEW SQUARE BUILT
ABOVE AN UNDERGROUND CAR PARK.

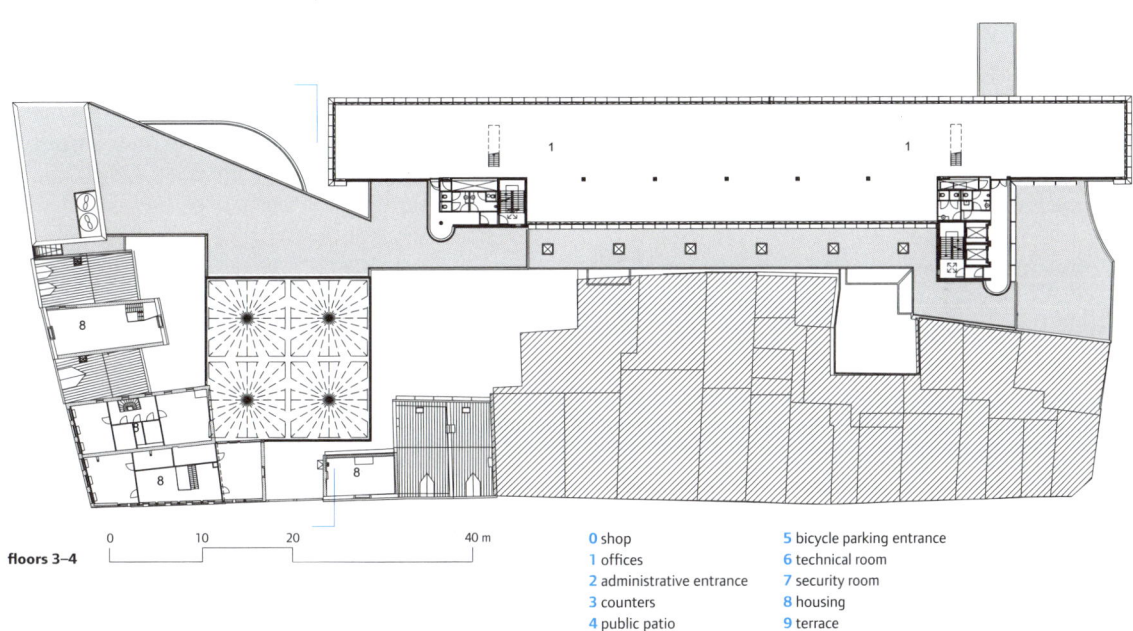

floors 3–4

0 10 20 40 m

0 shop	**5** bicycle parking entrance
1 offices	**6** technical room
2 administrative entrance	**7** security room
3 counters	**8** housing
4 public patio	**9** terrace

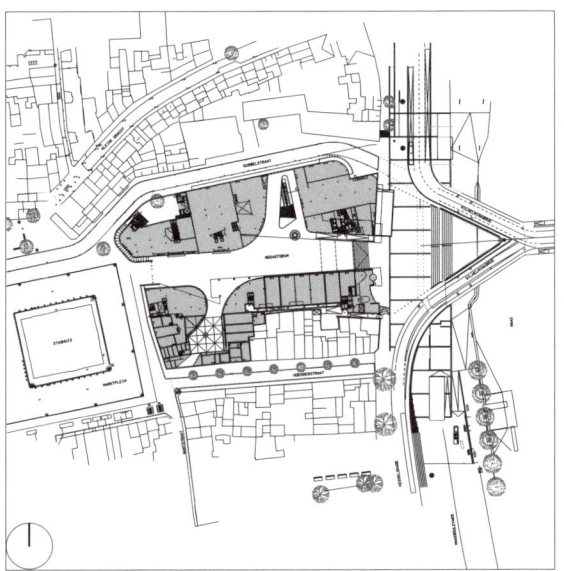

Mosae Forum

PROGRAMME business and administrative district
PROCEDURE originally a competition, later a collaboration
ARCHITECT Jo Coenen (northern part) |
Bruno Albert and Snelder Vola Petit (southern part)
CLIENT 3W Vastgoed Maastricht
LANDSCAPE ARCHITECT Jo Coenen STABILITY Arcadis
STRUCTURAL WORK | CARPENTRY | FAÇADE |
ELECTRICITY | HEATING BAM
AREA 8000 m² offices | 4500 m² shops | 7 apartments
COMPLETED 2007
www.brunoalbert.be

HESSENBERG URBAN DENSIFICATION
NIJMEGEN | NETHERLANDS
AWG | BIQ | MTD

TEXT Thomas Martin
PHOTOGRAPHY Stefan Müller

It is not awg architecten that sought to export itself, but rather the other way around. That bOb Van Reeth has often been invited to the Netherlands since the 1970s to teach, deliver talks and sit on juries certainly had something to do with it. In the early 1990s, then, the Dutch were looking beyond their borders for answers to a building problem about which local architects, due to the nature of their training, were clueless. Attempts had been made to solve the need for housing with suburban building, but that was a dead end. Belgium was the perfect choice: southern-influenced but not too exotic ideas, and with no language barrier. Urban densification commissions (with the typical commerce-housing tandem) were piling up for awg architecten.

Although the growth of awg mainly depends on the Dutch portfolio (up to 85% a couple of years ago), an office was never opened in the Netherlands. This is due to the favourable location of Antwerp, a two-hour drive from the Netherlands, Germany or France. "In the meantime, awg is already coming home", says Christine de Ruijter. "The Dutch housing market has less to offer, and in Belgium now there is a greater demand for architects with experience in inner-city development. Seen retrospectively, we were exporting ourselves in order better to be able to import: we have kept investing deliberately in Belgium". The firm often receives international commissions directly, through a vast and reliable network: "We once worked with a Dublin office in the Netherlands. When we later applied to build the Belgian embassy in Dublin, that connection settled it. The desire to collaborate generates trust: for clients it means less risk, and the authorities are grateful when you pass on commissions to local partners. Another reason for not wanting to do the complete project monitoring per se is that we can remain compact".

The Hessenberg project in Nijmegen is exemplary in this respect. When the winning but totally unsuitable concept of the Europe-wide competition for that location was unanimously rejected by local residents, they turned to awg architecten because a comparable inner-city project on the Mariaplaats in Utrecht had been well received in 1997. During the master-plan phase, the team had to coordinate a workshop discussion between two firms with very different styles, wary residents' groups, building contractors, and a handful of critical experts. A lot of time and energy went into communications and gaining back trust. As Filip Delanghe explains: "As a foreign firm, you are in a privileged neutral position. Everyone wants to show you the ropes in matters of Dutch building regulations. The Dutch are generally also better prepared and have more experience with large-scale projects. In Belgium architects are expected to find out everything themselves, whereas in the Netherlands a municipal project manager gathers all questions and contacts".

The firm successfully completed the commission, and that is rewarded in the Netherlands. More so than in Belgium, clients are inclined to call on you again. However, Christine de Ruijter and Filip Delanghe have noticed a decrease in that type of commissioning, and not only in the Netherlands. "The crisis has been a source of panic, there is no more vision, and only money talks. More and more projects look alike. They are no longer the result of contextual and historical research and discussion, but the rash result of a culture of competition".

Although it wasn't really their intention, since the early 1990s awg architecten has shifted more and more of its activities to the Netherlands. The Dutch were tired of firms that drew faster than their shadow and were looking for a firm that was really ready to listen.

HESSENBERG URBAN DENSIFICATION
NIJMEGEN | NETHERLANDS
AWG | **BIQ** | **MTD**

IT IS NOT AWG ARCHITECTEN THAT
SOUGHT TO EXPORT ITSELF, BUT RATHER
THE OTHER WAY AROUND.

HESSENBERG URBAN DENSIFICATION
NIJMEGEN | NETHERLANDS
AWG | BIQ | MTD

profile AA

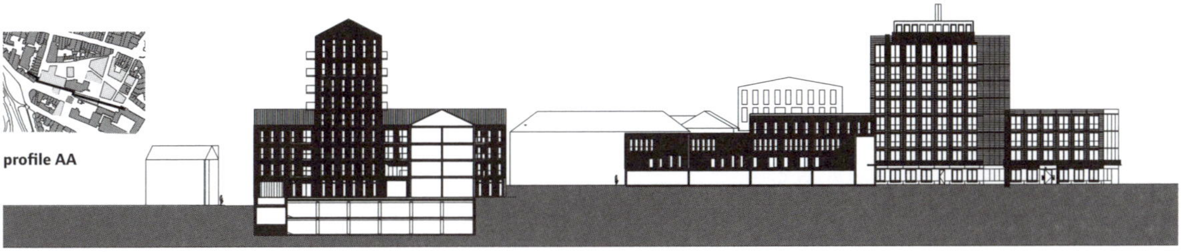

0 10 20 40 m

profile BB

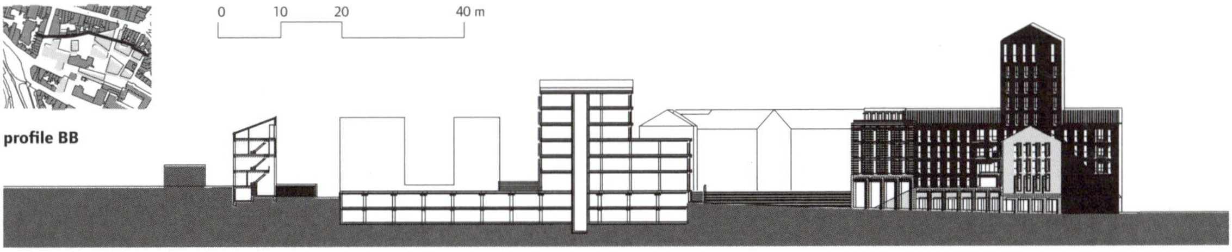

profile CC

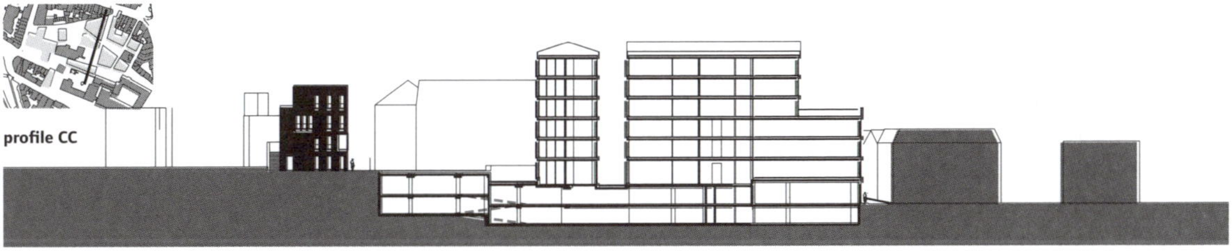

Hessenberg urban densification

PROGRAMME 191 apartments, 1200 m² shopping area,
two underground car parks including 225 parking spaces
CLIENT Heijmans Vastgoed | Hendriks Bouw en Ontwikkeling
ARCHITECT | URBANIST awg architecten
INVITED ARCHITECT biq stadsontwerp
LANDSCAPE ARCHITECT MTD Landschapsarchitecten
STABILITY Goudstikker – de Vries
TECHNIQUES | ACOUSTICS | EPB visietech
BUILDING CONTRACTOR Heijmans Vastgoed |
Hendriks Bouw en Ontwikkeling AREA 24 071 m²
BUDGET (excluding VAT and fees) 23 000 000 euro
COMPLETED June 2010
www.awg.be

BAIYUN INTERNATIONAL CONVENTION CENTRE

GUANGZHOU | CHINA

BURO II

TEXT Gilles Béchet
PHOTOGRAPHY Philippe van Gelooven

"We embarked on the adventure because we wanted to grow on the international stage. It is only once we had won the competition that we started wondering how we were going to get it done…", explains Pieterjan Vermoortel of Buro II. For an architectural firm that was, all things considered, relatively modest and had never built anything outside Belgium, the challenge was gigantic. They had to design a 300 000 m² building to house a convention centre in Guangzhou in the province of Guangdong in the south of China. "Within hardly a month we were present on site with a team of experts". In order to successfully complete this vast project within the set deadline, Buro II set up a mirror organization, in which each partner, the client and a Chinese architectural firm, formed a multidisciplinary team. Thanks to this open and participative modus operandi, they managed to exchange ideas and information that were both immediately integrated, thus ensuring the quality and speed of the work. On site, the Buro II team made use of the services of other Belgian firms specializing in the calculation of structural stability, acoustics, durability, energy management and landscaping. "Construction lasted 18 months, and throughout that time the Chinese teams in charge of the execution could consult us whenever a problem arose". Established in a development area in the north of the city, the convention centre had to establish a link between the urban agglomeration and the nearby mountains. In its project, Buro II had proposed to divide the buildings into five volumes so that they would blend in with the mountain ranges, while a system of eco-bridges made it possible to cross the urban motorway that cut off the site from its natural surroundings. Throughout the project, the Belgian team soaked up the local culture, at times quite unexpectedly, discovering for instance that the division into five buildings echoed a local legend as well as the Five Elements of Chinese philosophy. On the other hand, the use of red sandstone as a covering material was linked directly to the colour of the earth in that region, just as the texture of the façade refers to the jade plaques that covered the mummy of the emperor discovered in a nearby tomb. "Our client later told us that we had designed a project that was culturally Chinese. I think it's because we Belgians don't believe we know everything and are able to listen". The Guangzhou convention centre has had a lot of positive repercussions for Buro II. Several Belgian companies setting up shop in China have asked them to build their factories. The firm has also taken part in other competitions, even though, in the case of the Centre of Science and Technology in Nanning, the Buro II project, which received first prize, was, for obscure reasons, dismissed in favour of another project. Nevertheless, working on the convention centre in an entirely different culture was, Pieterjan Vermoortel concludes, "a wonderful experience for us, and we learned a lot from the Chinese and their sense of organization".

Although the firm had never built outside Belgium, Buro II won the competition for an imposing convention centre in Guangzhou, China. Designed and built in record time, the project was successfully completed thanks to the creation of a mirror organization run by the client and a local architectural firm.

BAIYUN INTERNATIONAL CONVENTION CENTRE
GUANGZHOU | CHINA
BURO II

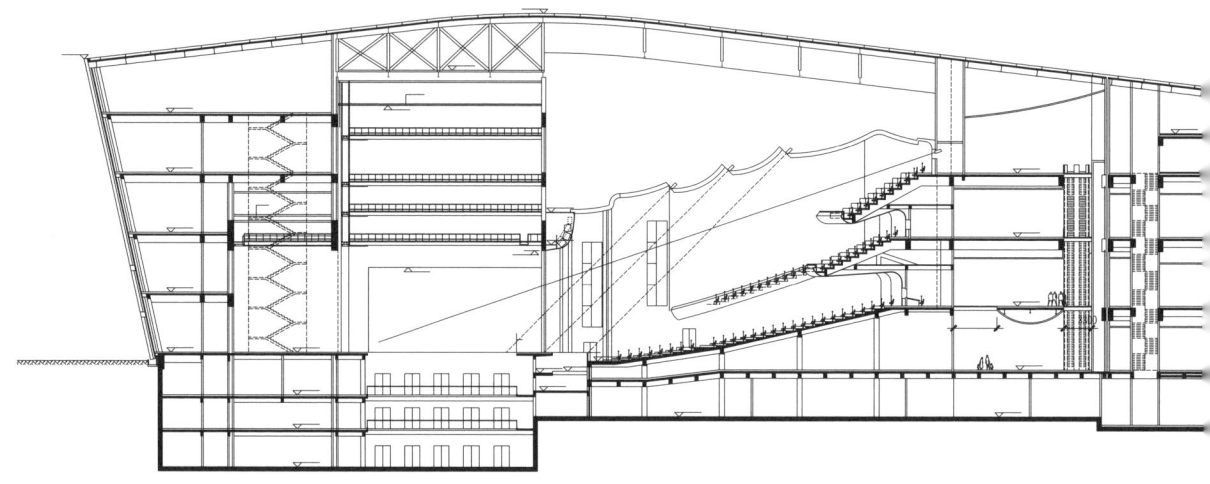

**conference hall,
longitudinal section**

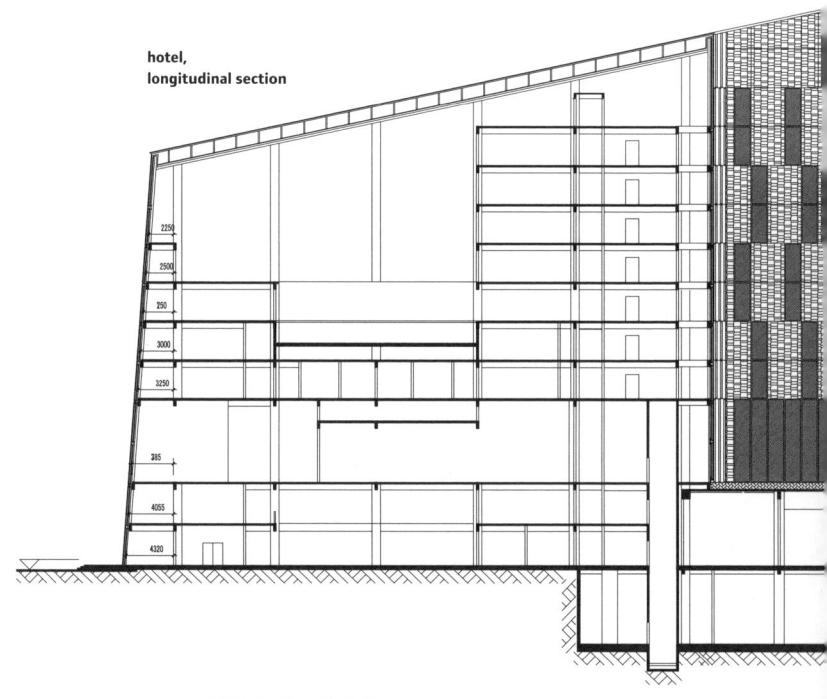

**hotel,
longitudinal section**

TO COMPLETE THIS VAST PROJECT WITHIN
THE DEADLINE, BURO II SET UP A MIRROR
ORGANIZATION, IN WHICH EACH PARTNER, THE
CLIENT AND A CHINESE ARCHITECTURAL FIRM,
FORMED A MULTIDISCIPLINARY TEAM.

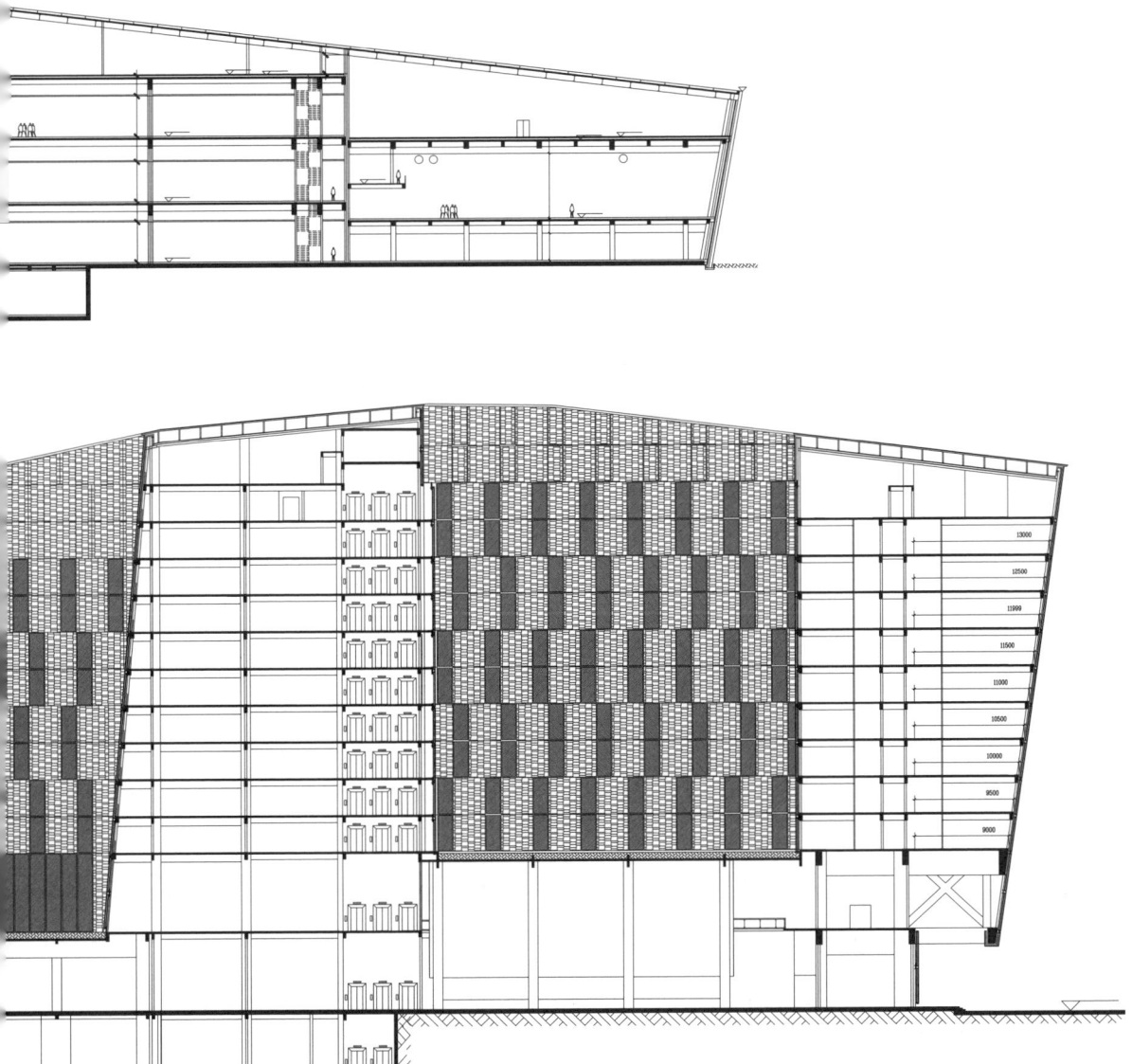

ECONOMIC ACTIVITY

OUR CLIENT LATER TOLD US THAT WE HAD
DESIGNED A PROJECT THAT WAS CULTURALLY
CHINESE. I THINK IT'S BECAUSE WE BELGIANS
DON'T BELIEVE WE KNOW EVERYTHING AND
ARE ABLE TO LISTEN.

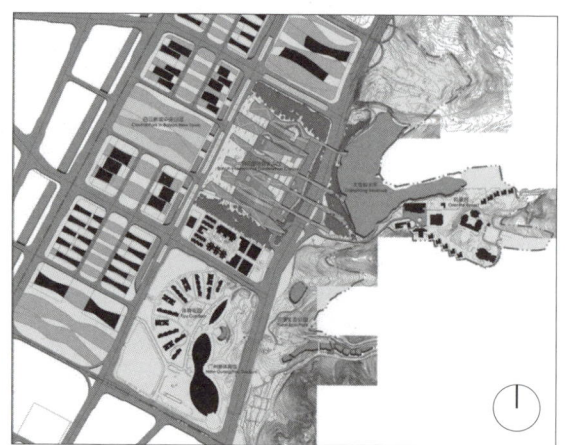

Baiyun International Convention Centre

PROGRAMME congress centre for national and international conferences
PROCEDURE international competition
ARCHITECT Buro II in collaboration with Design Institute of CITIC China
CLIENT Guangzhou Baiyun International Conference Centre
LANDSCAPE ARCHITECT Denis Dujardin | Stefaan Thiers
STABILITY Ney & Partners TECHNIQUES Ingenium
ENERGY | ACOUSTICS Daidalos Peutz FAÇADE Van Santen & Ass
INTERIOR LENS°ASS THEATRE TECHNIQUES T.T.A.S.
AREA 272 000 m² BUDGET (excluding VAT and fees) 315 000 000 euro
COMPLETED January 2007
www.b2ai.com

System 800
Comfort to Care

hewi.com

Innovative System Solutions for Generations: an universal sanitary system, available in chrome and polyamide, offers a broad range of use. System 800 includes sanitary accessories, comfort and convenience elements, accessibility products, washbasins and mirrors. System 800 is universal – it is suitable for use both in the private bathroom and for fitting out hotels or commercial buildings.

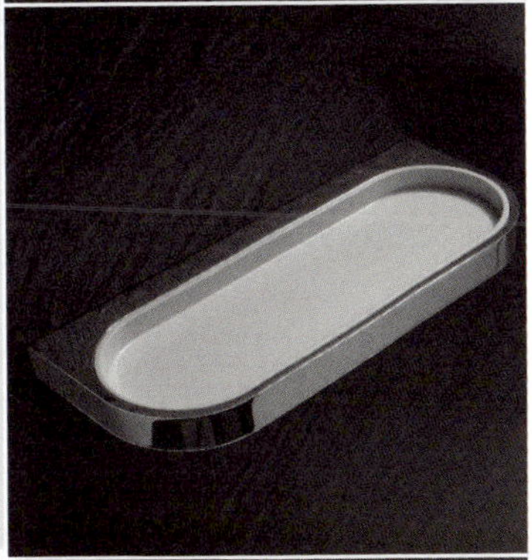

FENCHURCH FACTORY EXPANSION
SUZHOU | CHINA
PLUSOFFICEARCHITECTS

TEXT Cécile Vandernoot
PHOTOGRAPHY Bart Mahieu

Headed by Ward Verbakel and Nathan Ooms, the Brussels-based firm plusofficearchitects collaborates with different teams (trained through their network of relations) on international architecture or urban-planning projects and competitions. They have built abroad since the opening of the firm five years ago, and a second office under the same name has opened in China, managed by their friend and colleague Bart Mahieu. This geographic specificity has attracted European companies wishing to build in China and looking for better quality services than those allegedly found on the local market. Bart Mahieu, who now resides in Shanghai, has followed intensive training courses to learn both the local language and building techniques. "The city of Suzhou is especially known for its historic centre and canals. The industrial area in the suburbs is growing haphazardly. There is no master plan in China, no set of town-planning regulations to help guide you or, on the contrary, put a spoke in your wheel. The chosen approach depends solely on your own analysis of the urban context, the land and the stakes". The Fenchurch factory, where medical filters are made, wished to expand its only production hall by creating a 4800 m² extension on a budget of less than 150 euro/m² (including the cost of technical equipment). The additional volume was meant to accommodate an assembly hall, a canteen, a double-height production hall, a 'clean room', and a laboratory. The important task of organizing the complex structure was like assembling a jigsaw puzzle. The formal composition of the building follows the functional logic of stacking. The building section can be seen in the façade, for instance, while certain protruding elements pick up the heights of the existing structure. The build-ing's marked horizontality is shrewdly punctuated by the vertical frames of the openings – frames which are, moreover, of a standard format and were produced locally. "The building is low-tech and thermally insulated, which is not very common. We thought it was important to make modest innovations. In China, the companies that build are seeking to improve their image. Their desire to import

Western-style quality and design is quite common, but in this case, the building stands out in its category because it draws its strength mainly from local technologies and materials".
While the firm is now used to handling relatively large-scale projects, it also deals with smaller undertakings in Belgium. The approach remains fundamentally the same, however. Concept, structure and programming are analyzed in detail and formulated schematically. This visually effective communication is notably due to the language incompatibilities with which the architects have been confronted in the past.

Plusofficearchitects is responsible for the expansion of a factory in the industrial area of Suzhou in China. Using local building techniques, the firm adopted a new formal grammar in line with the existing structure.

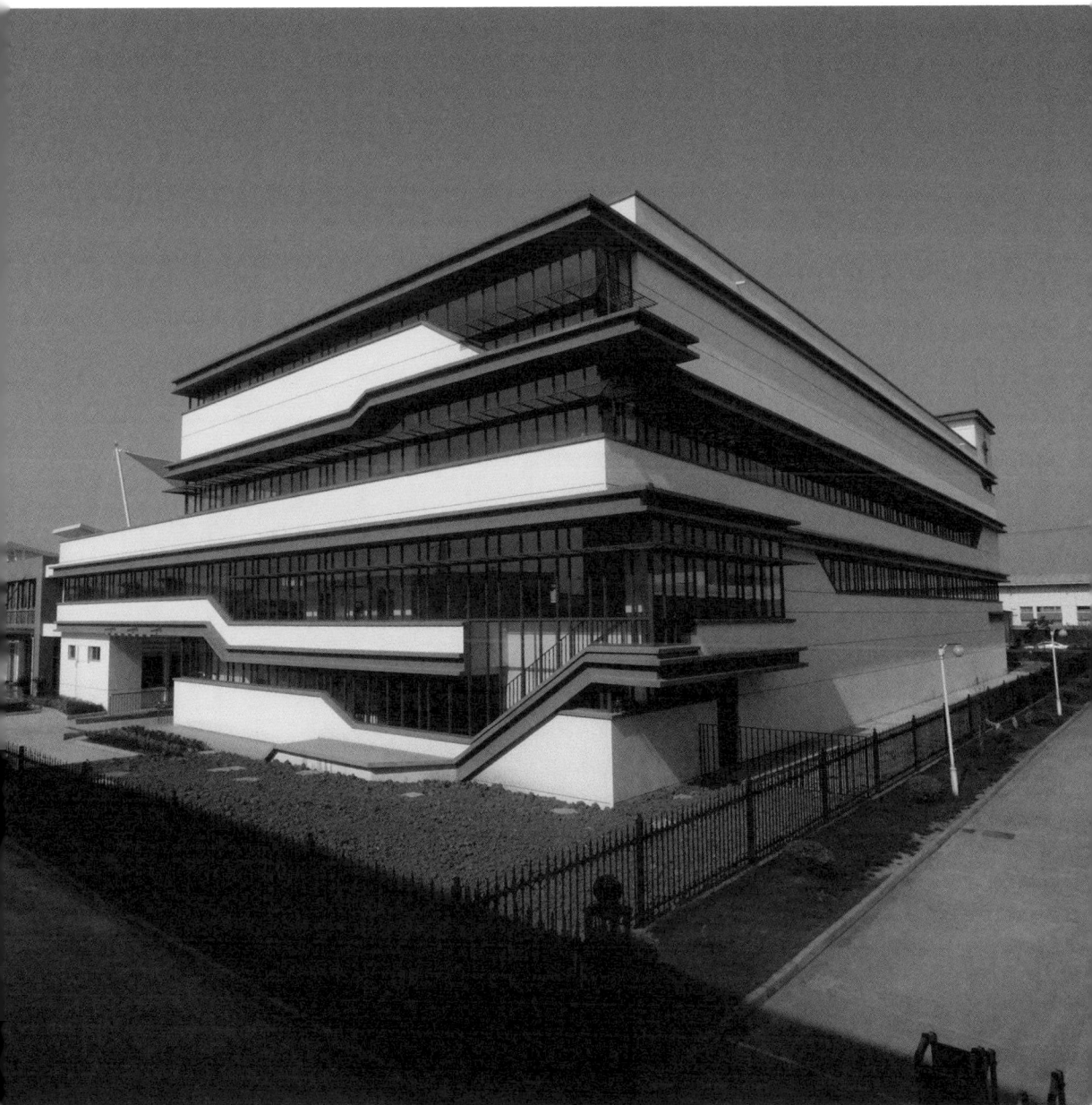

FENCHURCH FACTORY EXPANSION
SUZHOU | CHINA
PLUSOFFICEARCHITECTS

THE BUILDING'S MARKED HORIZONTALITY IS
SHREWDLY PUNCTUATED BY THE VERTICAL
FRAMES OF THE OPENINGS.

Fenchurch production facility and offices

PROGRAMME extension of an existing factory building with
offices, a laboratory space, a 'clean room' and production space
PROCEDURE private order
ARCHITECT plusofficearchitects
CLIENT Fenchurch Filters Suzhou Ltd.
CALL FOR TENDERS & CONSTRUCTION SUPERVISION
Plus Office Consulting China
STABILITY | TECHNIQUES | ACOUSTICS | EPB
Suzhou City Architecture Design Institute Co.
STRUCTURAL WORK | CARPENTRY | FAÇADE | ELECTRICITY | HEATING |
WORKMANSHIP OF INTERIOR Wuxi No. 5 Construction Company
AREA 4800 m² COMPLETED February 2007
www.plusoffice.eu

LE PIN WINERY
POMEROL | FRANCE
ROBBRECHT EN DAEM ARCHITECTEN

TEXT Audrey Contesse
PHOTOGRAPHY Robbrecht en Daem Architecten

"If we look at the entirety of the firm's productions abroad, a red thread soon emerges, and that is art", says Paul Robbrecht. "We are very interested in art, and it is our connections with the art world that brought us these commissions". The first international architectural project for Robbrecht en Daem Architecten, a firm founded in 1975, was that of the Aue pavilions at documenta in Kassel (1992-94), of which fellow Belgian Jan Hoet was the director. These pavilions were later taken down and reassembled in Almere: "We thus received some visibility in the Netherlands, and conversely, we developed an interest in the Netherlands". In 1996, the firm took part in the competition for the extension of the Boijmans Van Beuningen Museum in Rotterdam, which it won. "The museum's programme appealed to us, and the director, Chris Dercon, a fellow Belgian, also encouraged our participation". After a brief incursion into Switzerland, it is in England that the architects then intervened with two projects conducted in parallel. One was the result of an international competition by invitation: the expansion of the Whitechapel Gallery in London (2003-09). The second was a direct commission: two observation towers constructed along a bicycle path. One of these 'High Views' is located in Lincoln, the other in Boston. "Lincoln is a medieval city like Bruges, and it was during the establishment of a partnership between the two cities that the client discovered the Concertgebouw in Bruges, and then contacted us". The firm's first project in France was completed in the spring of 2011: the Le Pin winery in Pomerol, near Bordeaux. "It belongs to one of the 30 members of a Belgian family established in the region". One can thus say that another red thread running through their foreign projects is the Belgian network abroad. "We were initially contacted for an opinion, but then, one thing led to another, and soon we were given the commission. As with each project outside Belgium, we relied on a local person who could handle administrative issues and, in this case, was an expert in winery management. We had to do a lot of research, since viticulture is a very technical art".

At present, 20% of the firm's commissions come from abroad, and the team is increasingly taking part in international competitions – not out of financial considerations, but in order to discover themes and challenges that move and interest them. Next to their architectural productions, the exhibition Pacing Through Architecture has been touring the world since 2009 (UK, South Africa, France): "Even if it is not potential clients who visit the exhibition, it can lead to intellectually enriching encounters which can in turn bring in new commissions".

An interest in art led the Ghent-based firm Robbrecht en Daem Architecten to come in contact with the international art world and also stimulated their commissions abroad. Underlying this approach is the team's intellectual curiosity.

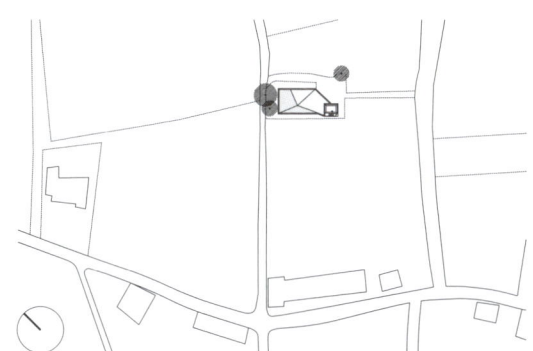

LE PIN WINERY
POMEROL | FRANCE
ROBBRECHT EN DAEM ARCHITECTEN

AS WITH EACH PROJECT OUTSIDE BELGIUM,
WE RELIED ON A LOCAL PERSON WHO COULD
HANDLE ADMINISTRATIVE ISSUES AND, IN THIS
CASE, WAS AN EXPERT IN WINERY MANAGEMENT.

LE PIN WINERY
POMEROL | FRANCE
ROBBRECHT EN DAEM ARCHITECTEN

THE TEAM IS INCREASINGLY TAKING PART IN
INTERNATIONAL COMPETITIONS IN ORDER TO
DISCOVER THEMES AND CHALLENGES THAT
MOVE AND INTEREST THEM.

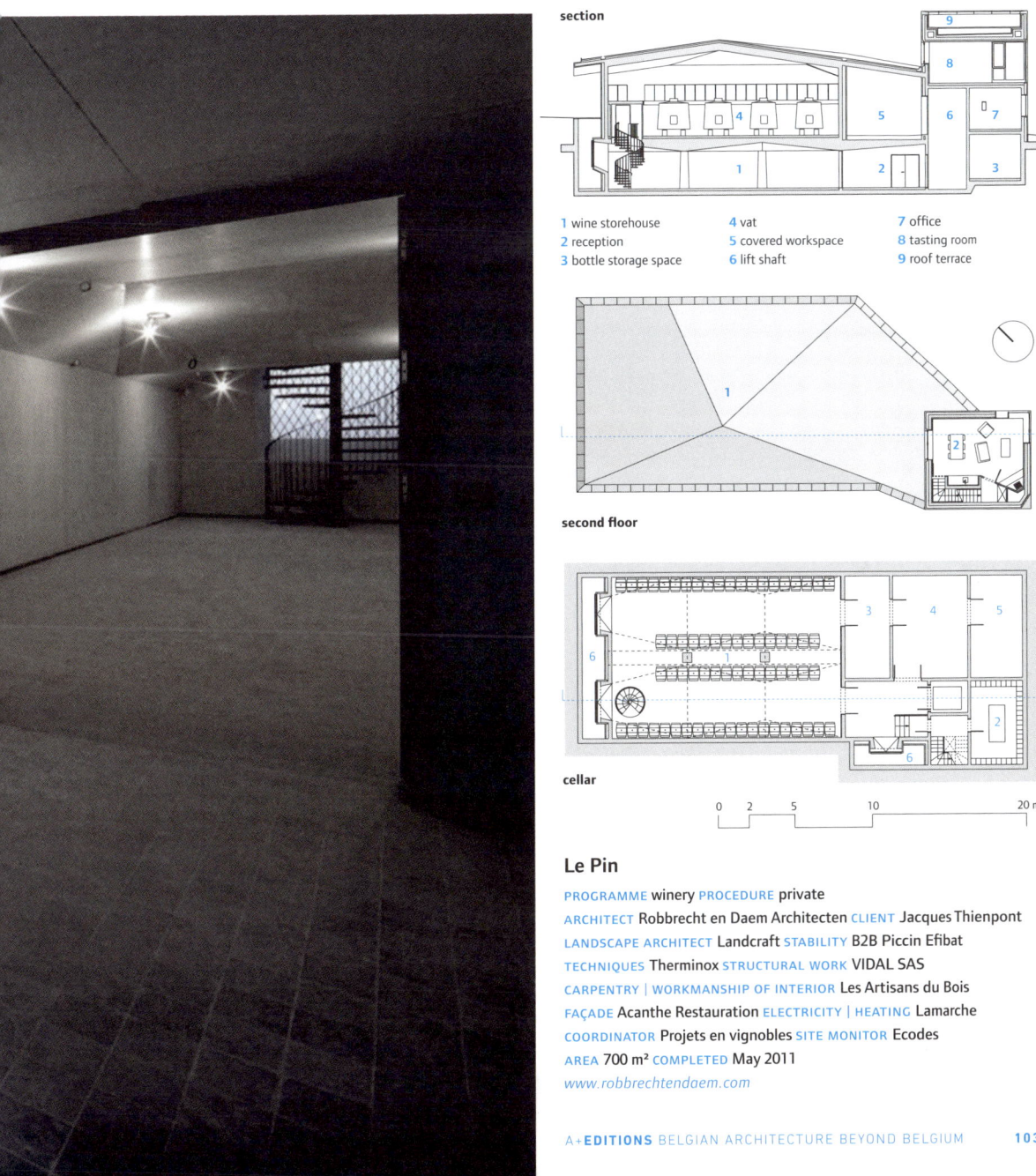

section

1 wine storehouse
2 reception
3 bottle storage space

4 vat
5 covered workspace
6 lift shaft

7 office
8 tasting room
9 roof terrace

second floor

cellar

0   2   5   10   20 m

Le Pin

PROGRAMME winery PROCEDURE private
ARCHITECT Robbrecht en Daem Architecten CLIENT Jacques Thienpont
LANDSCAPE ARCHITECT Landcraft STABILITY B2B Piccin Efibat
TECHNIQUES Therminox STRUCTURAL WORK VIDAL SAS
CARPENTRY | WORKMANSHIP OF INTERIOR Les Artisans du Bois
FAÇADE Acanthe Restauration ELECTRICITY | HEATING Lamarche
COORDINATOR Projets en vignobles SITE MONITOR Ecodes
AREA 700 m² COMPLETED May 2011
www.robbrechtendaem.com

Image © Concept and Analysis Studio Fall 2011 KULeuven (C.Furlan, N.Aernouts, J.De Maeyer, T.T.V. Pham)

MASTER OF URBANISM AND STRATEGIC PLANNING

MASTER OF HUMAN SETTLEMENTS

The Department of Architecture, Urbanism and Planning of the KULeuven presents 2 post-graduate programs. The 2 semester Master of Human Settlements focuses on urbanism and planning in developed and developing countries world wide [www.asro.kuleuven.be/mahs] The 4 semester Master of Urbanism and Strategic Planning pursues a critical understanding of the contemporary conditions of urban regions and cities across the globe [www.asro.kuleuven.be/mausp]. MaUSP is participating in EMU, the European Master of Urbanism organised by IUA Venice, UPC Barcelona, TU Delft and KULeuven [www.emurbanism.eu]. **FOR EU-citizens, applications for the year 2012-2013 are open until the 1st of June 2012** More information? Contact maura.slootmaekers@asro.kuleuven.be, tel +32 (0)16 32 13 91, fax +32 (0)16 32 19 81 Department of Architecture, Urbanism and Planning, Oude Molen 00.21, Kasteelpark Arenberg 51, B3001 Heverlee, Belgium

MaUSP MAHS

KATHOLIEKE UNIVERSITEIT LEUVEN

european postgraduate masters in urbanism strategies and design for cities and territories

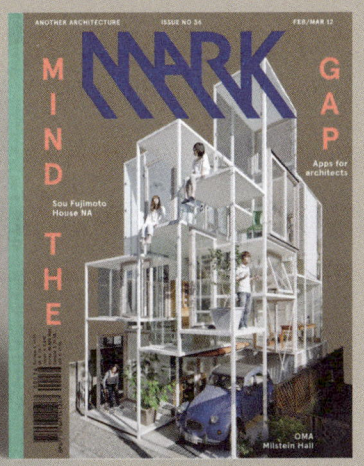

RANGUEIL HOSPITAL
TOULOUSE | FRANCE
ART & BUILD | SÉQUENCES

TEXT Gilles Béchet
PHOTOGRAPHY Vincent Boutin

Although 50% of the revenue of the Brussels-based architectural firm Art & Build is generated abroad, 80% of production is still carried out in Brussels. "For our operations outside Belgium, we always enter into a partnership with a local office that can act as a technical and administrative go-between. Conversely, we offer the same service to outside firms that are building in Brussels", says David Roulin, architect and senior partner. France, where the firm has two offices, constitutes its first export market. In order to build up its reputation there, Art & Build took the time to discover the country over a period of three or four years in order to show itself, take part in competitions and establish contacts. Resting on 11 partners, the firm can afford to devote four of them to France. Often canvassing the country in tandem with Belgian property developers, the architects are aware that their approach is unanimously appreciated. "Prospective clients recognize our eye for detail as well as our sense of dialogue and discussion, where French architects are often more bullish". Present in Paris for more than ten years, Art & Build was waiting for the right moment to establish itself in the south of the country, where several projects were brewing. The turning point came when the firm won the competition to build a new technical capacity on the site of the Rangueil hospital in Toulouse. Established in the 'pink city' since 2007, the Art & Build office on location employs four members of staff and covers a territory extending from Bordeaux to Montpellier. "It takes time to set oneself up in a city and be recognized as a real local, but we wouldn't have done this just anywhere", explains Gilles Bourgeois, the regional director.

Constructed above the main entrance to the site dating from the 1970s, the new building consists of four floors, two of which are reserved for the operating theatres. Drawing on their experience in the hospital sector, Art & Build here refined the 'forward flow' principle, i.e., a circulation system organized according to the level of cleanliness (from the cleanest to the dirtiest). In order to harmonize the exterior and blend in with the older brick buildings, the cement envelope was clad with a terracotta structure, which notably helps protect the interior from direct sunlight.

Upon completion of the Rangueil site, the Toulouse office took on the coordination of two sets of housing projects in Montpellier, which, as ever, were developed in Brussels but had been initiated by the Paris office. In association with Bouygues, the firm also obtained another hospital project to be built on the site of the former AZF factory. "The visibility of our first projects as well as our commercial dynamism nationwide contributed to our notoriety, meaning that key players in the public buildings and works sector now call on us to participate with them in ambitious design and realization operations", concludes David Roulin.

Rangueil hospital

PROGRAMME technical capacity with four levels (operating theatres, intensive care and ongoing care unit, burns unit, main security post)
PROCEDURE competitive tender for urban project management (procurement contracts) separate trade contractor market
ARCHITECT Art & Build Architect | Séquences
CLIENT university hospital CHU Toulouse
STABILITY Sotec Ingénierie TECHNIQUES SNC-Lavalin
STRUCTURAL WORK Eiffage | MAS CARPENTRY Realco
FAÇADE Sopocome ELECTRICITY Forclum | Snef HEATING Snef CVC
WORKMANSHIP OF INTERIOR ETP AREA 13 000 m² (net floor area)
BUDGET (excluding VAT and fees, work excluding equipment)
32 000 000 euro COMPLETED June 2011
www.artbuild.eu

Very active abroad, not least in France, the architectural firm Art & Build likes to set up local offices as soon as there is sufficient activity. This was the case when the firm won the competition for the Rangueil hospital in Toulouse.

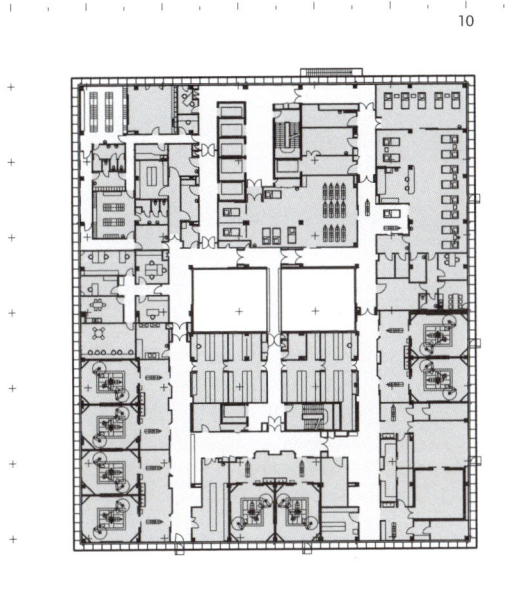

10   0

10 —

typical floor (above), and layout (below)

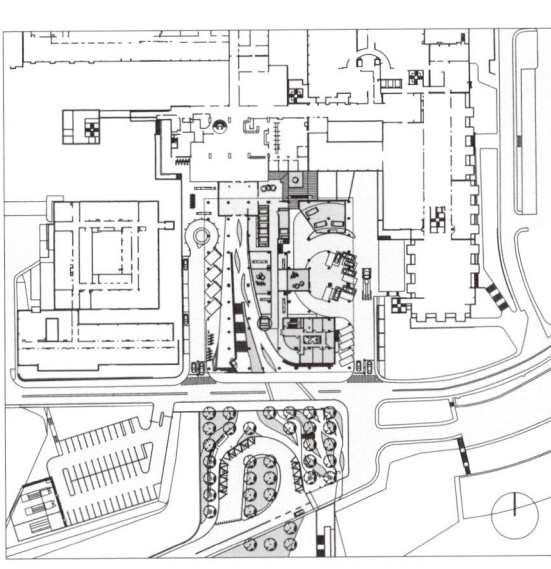

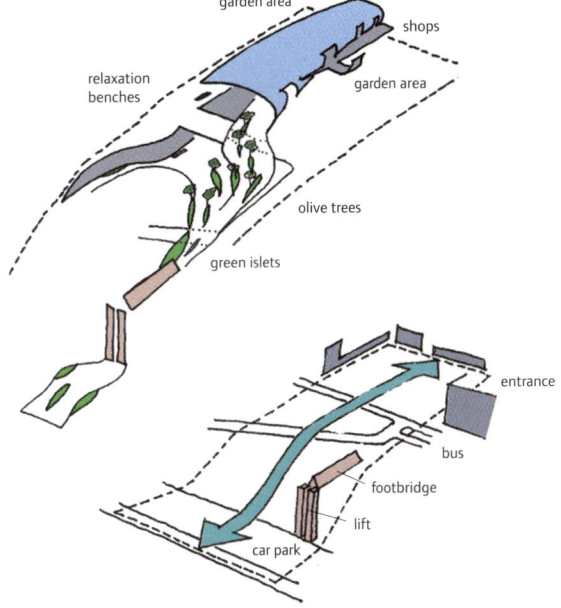

garden area
shops
relaxation benches
garden area
olive trees
green islets
entrance
bus
footbridge
lift
car park

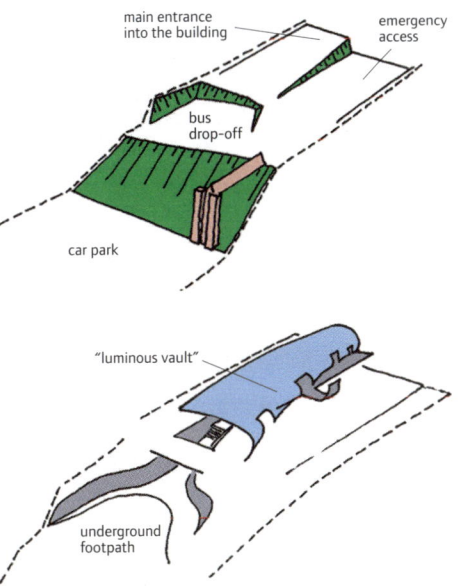

main entrance into the building
emergency access
bus drop-off
car park

"luminous vault"

underground footpath

HEALTHCARE

ART & BUILD TOOK THE TIME TO DISCOVER THE COUNTRY OVER A PERIOD OF THREE OR FOUR YEARS IN ORDER TO SHOW ITSELF, TAKE PART IN COMPETITIONS AND ESTABLISH CONTACTS.

VINMEC INTERNATIONAL HOSPITAL
HANOI | VIETNAM
VK

TEXT Thomas Martin
PHOTOGRAPHY VK

Ten years ago the engineering and architectural firm VK decided to focus increasingly on healthcare. Ever since the construction of its first hospital in Aalst (1985), much expertise has been acquired and VK keeps receiving more and more similar commissions. With four offices and 250 members of staff, of which 60 architects, VK has a large market share in Belgium. The firm wanted to grow further, however, but that had become difficult in Belgium and Europe. The market was saturated and there was too much competition.

In 2009 VK launched a business development department, which was to work out an international growth strategy and thus went in search of politically stable developing countries that had not yet been overrun. A partnership was set up in Vietnam with dwp, but things did not go smoothly and VK soon decided to set up its own office, with six local collaborators. In Russia, on the other hand, the firm is working in partnership with a local office on a master plan for a hospital with 2000 beds. And for work on the National Library of Kazakhstan, the firm is collaborating with a firm that has been bought over and is now under Belgian control.

What makes this work abroad possible? VK is smaller and thus more flexible and cheaper than the large US companies that are ubiquitous, and the above healthcare expertise is also a major asset in developing countries. Kenneth Groosman, business director for healthcare, explains: "You don't just get that kind of commission immediately. Our experience and interest in the subject have convinced clients: we organized conferences with Belgian speakers and established contacts, also through the embassies. That makes it easier for people to choose you. In Vietnam, moreover, there is little competition and a big need for hospitals. There is ample funding, both from the private and public sector. And let's not forget that Belgium is recognized worldwide as a country that is far ahead in healthcare matters". Even though public funds are involved, the building process is a lot smoother than in Belgium. "There are less building site

regulations, and apparently some 3000 workers worked 24/7. It went incredibly fast: the cement wasn't even dry when they were already busy plastering and laying cable troughs. We did the entire design, but that's where our mission stopped. As regards materials and execution, local companies can do as they please. That building culture does not quite resemble our own, and that demands quite some empathy. In Belgium you first meet with experts and department heads, but in Vietnam or Russia the client will give you a general commission – and the details are up to you".

By 2015 VK hopes to generate a third of its revenue abroad, and it is well on its way to meeting this objective. The company in Vietnam is now virtually breaking even. Groosman explains: "In the meantime we have also been exporting ourselves by other means: we are working on a teaching programme in hospital design for our Vietnamese colleagues. It's an absolute necessity, since the Vietnamese are not familiar with high-tech buildings in which everything is integrated".

For companies wishing to follow VK's example, Kenneth Groosman has some precious advice: "First do a thorough market analysis and build your relationships. Stick to your ethics and avoid improper practices: you will be better off building up a reputation for honesty. You also need capital and a healthy national cash flow. Whoever goes abroad to compensate for poor national results is ruined".

What can you get done in 13 months? In Belgium, you might just finish a sketch plan. But in a developing country in Asia, you can throw up a hospital with 500 beds. With loose building site regulations and a young population that is eager to work hard, is Vietnam a building paradise, or are things a bit more complicated?

VINMEC INTERNATIONAL HOSPITAL

HANOI | VIETNAM

VK

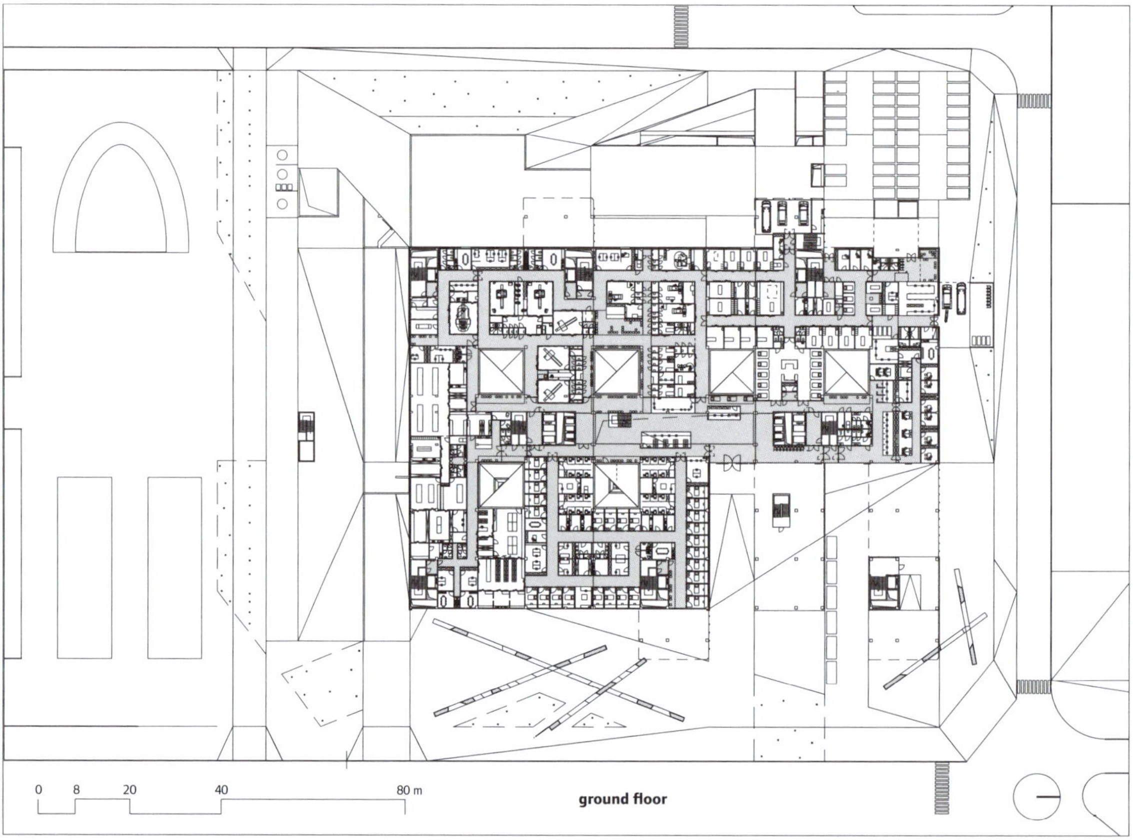

0 8 20 40 80 m

ground floor

VinMec International Hospital

PROGRAMME programming, architecture, building services, infrastructure, interior architecture PROCEDURE private tender
ARCHITECT VK CLIENT VinGroup STABILITY VinGroup
TECHNIQUES | ACOUSTICS | ENERGY CONCEPT VK
SURFACE 80 000 m² [above ground 54 000 m² | underground 26 000 m²] – 500 beds
BUDGET (excluding VAT and fees) 100 000 000 USD
COMPLETED January 2012
www.vingroup.vn | www.vkgroup.be

REALTY
Let's talk real estate

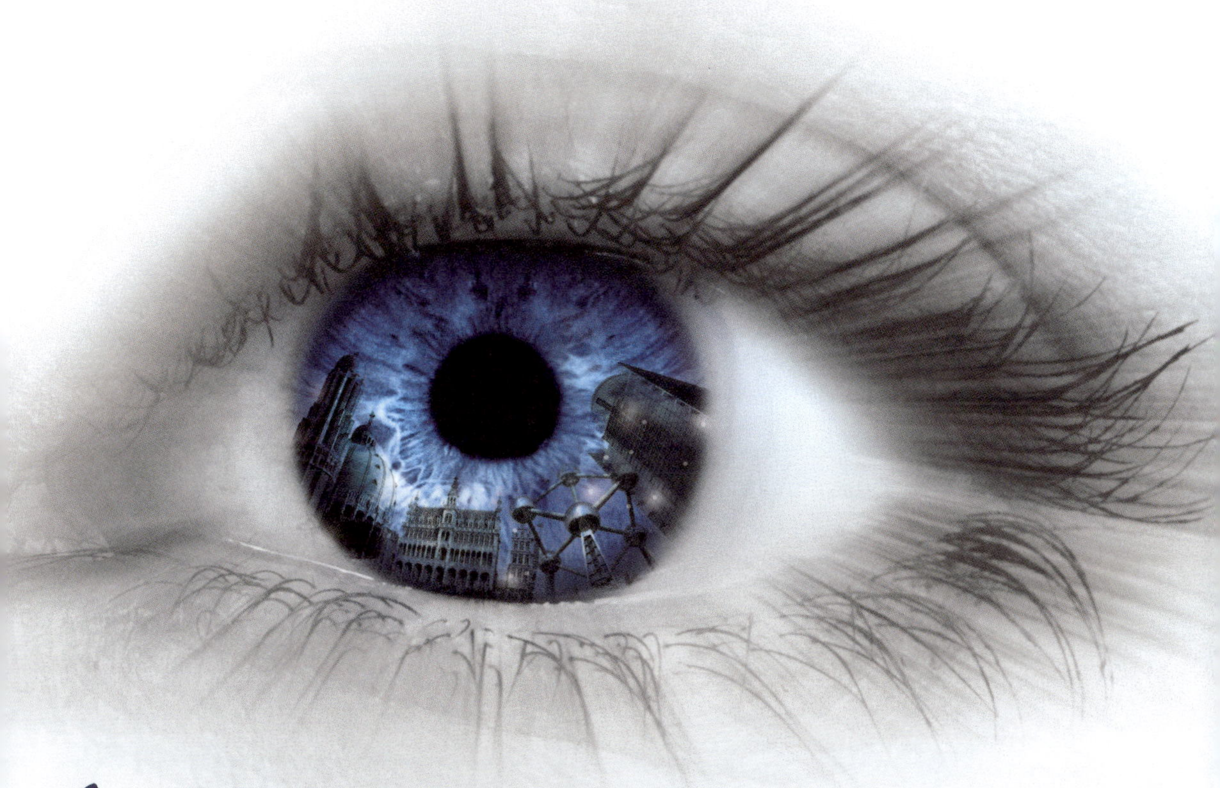

'

The real estate
investment view
from Europe's capital

22, 23 & 24 May 2012 | Tour & Taxis Brussels

www.realty-brussels.com

organised by **artexis**

UPSI-BVS

IFMA.
International Facility Management Association

DE TIJD

L'Echo

GREEN MANGO REFERENCE CENTRE
LUBUMBASHI | DEMOCRATIC REPUBLIC OF CONGO
PHILIPPE SAMYN AND PARTNERS

TEXT Gilles Béchet
PHOTOGRAPHY Philipe Samyn and Partners

"Masonry makes no sense in Central Africa. It is entirely alien to their culture". To design the building intended to house a shelter for destitute children in the region of Lubumbashi, Philippe Samyn opted for a construction method in line with local practices. A curious traveller, the architect was attracted by the extreme fertility of informal work during his many voyages across the continent. Why should one choose brickwork when their expertise in matters of woodwork and weaving is unmatched? And why rule out the use of ironwork when welding is so close to basketry? The Green Mango project consists of three long buildings framed by tree-lined patios. Their curved sheet-metal roofs rest on a structure consisting of welded wire mesh.

This project is neither the most prestigious nor the most imposing to have been designed by the architect for an international project, but it is highly symbolic. An alter-globalist at heart, Philippe Samyn decided in 2005 to devote part of his architectural firm's profits to offer 'ready-to-use' working drawings for worthwhile projects in developing countries. "I had participated, for various international institutions, in several large-scale projects that never materialized. I thus thought I would be more effective were I to offer drawings directly to those who could make good use of them". Having said this, finding projects that were likely to be realized was not as simple as expected. Neither a building for a school of architecture in Lubumbashi nor a community centre in Ngozi in Burundi saw the light, and it is ultimately a modest project that emerged in the middle of nowhere, supported by two frail ladies. The working drawings were handed over months ago already, but news from the road to Kipopo is scarce. To keep informed of the project's state of progress, the architects have been forced to go fishing for information, learning, in passing, that the sheet metal from South Africa has been replaced by local sheet metal and that the decision has been taken to add a brick wall to the project. "It is proof, on the one hand, that all this makes sense but also, on the other, that there are tremendous difficulties involved in implementing this type of project. These projects are like bottles cast out to sea. One throws a bottle out to sea without knowing when it will be picked up, before casting out another one, and then another".

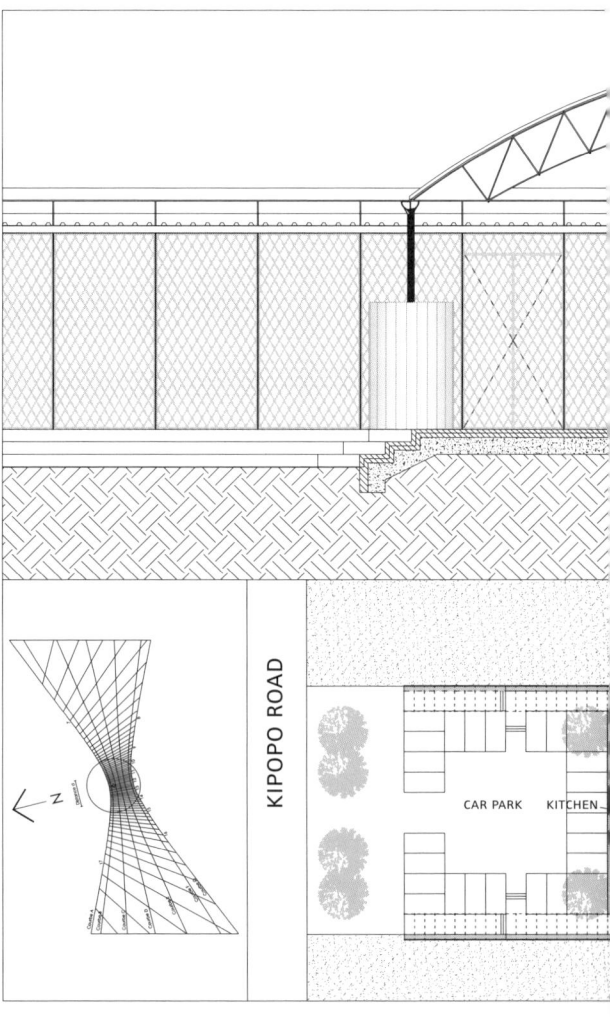

KIPOPO ROAD

CAR PARK   KITCHEN

In addition to his ambitious international projects, Philippe Samyn devotes part of his time to the preparation of working drawings offered to NGOs. A first project has seen the light in the Democratic Republic of Congo.

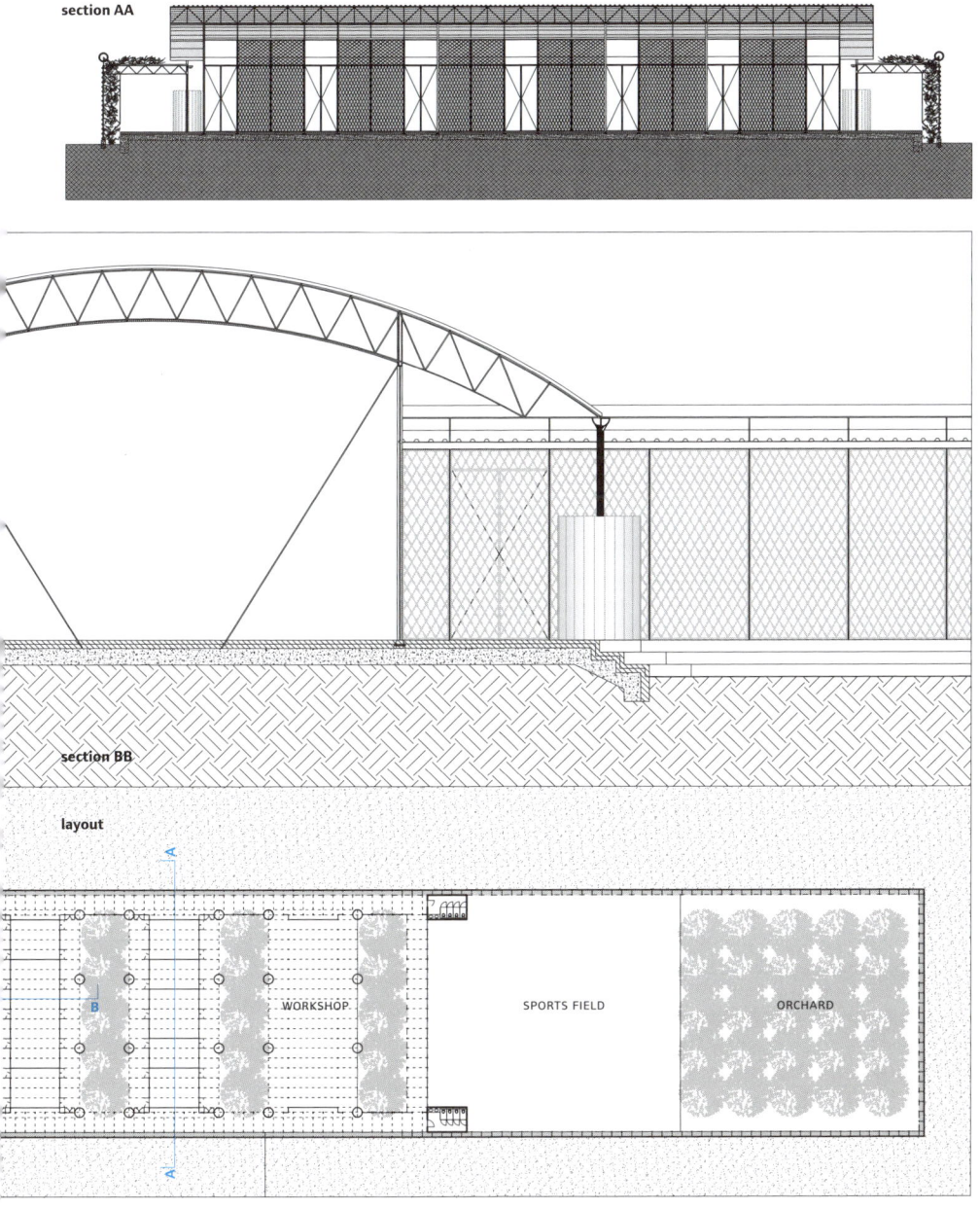

section AA

section BB

layout

WORKSHOP

SPORTS FIELD

ORCHARD

GREEN MANGO REFERENCE CENTRE
LUBUMBASHI | DEMOCRATIC REPUBLIC OF CONGO
PHILIPPE SAMYN AND PARTNERS

Green Mango reference centre

PROGRAMME a reference centre comprising four principle elements (main building with kitchen, studios, various other areas, parking zone, sports field, orchard) PROCEDURE private
ARCHITECT | LANDSCAPE ARCHITECT | STABILITY |
TECHNIQUES | ACOUSTICS Philippe Samyn and Partners
CLIENT Coup de Pouce STRUCTURAL WORK | CARPENTRY |
FAÇADE | ELECTRICITY self-construction
AREA 1250 m² COMPLETED ongoing
www.samynandpartners.be

BELGIAN ARCHITECTURE HAS UNDERGONE A RADICAL TRANSFORMATION OVER THE PAST 20 YEARS.

Arthur Wortmann

THE MOST RELEVANT COUNTRY IN EUROPE.

Harm Tilman

Editor in chief | de Architect

A serious debate is under way in the Netherlands over the extent to which we will have to tighten our belts. Other countries are trying to stimulate the economy by opening the money taps. The question remains as to what good this will do us. Luckily, a plan is glimmering on the horizon in the shape of a sketch: architecture in Belgium.

Let me explain what I mean.

In my opinion, we should now especially be thinking, reflecting, cycling and reading instead of driving at 130 kmh on the motorway, a measure which the Dutch government recently implemented with the help of a proposal that will swallow billions.

It is precisely now that the banking crisis has shaken our financial system to its core and housing construction has come to a standstill that we need architecture of breathtaking power and beauty. It should help us go deeper into reality. It is no longer a matter of ornamentation, influences and iconography. It is about resonance and the practice of our trade.

This goes against the architectonic culture currently at work in the Netherlands, still largely hooked on notions such as concept and research. And that is why Flanders is the Promised Land for the Dutch. For years already we have been attending more architecture exhibitions in de Singel in Antwerp than in the Netherlands Architecture Institute in Rotterdam. An added bonus is that the architecture itself is shown in Antwerp, in the form of ideas, drawings and sketches.

Everything we see there, we naturally take home with us. A respectable number of these Belgian architects have already built in the Netherlands: bOb van Reeth, Bruno Albert, Charles Vandenhove, Crepain & Binst, Laurent Ney, etc. But our interest goes beyond this. I'm thinking, for instance, of the town-planning policy in Antwerp, the Flemish Government Architect's Open Call and Master Examination, or the vision on infrastructure. All this makes Belgium a strong exporting country.

Why? Perhaps because Belgian architects are especially practice-oriented architects. This also holds for those building in the Netherlands. When these architects consider their trade, they reflect on how they build, the paths they take, how they imagine buildings on location, how they assemble the elements in relation to one another. This makes Belgium the most relevant country in Europe today.

For a number of years now the Belgian pavilion in the Giardini has regularly been numbered among the positive surprises of the Venice Architecture Biennale. It has become impossible to overlook the fact that an independent architecture has developed in this country. The remarkable thing here is not just this fact, per se, but also that this architecture is supported by both the public purse and private investors. Architecture does not drop from the sky. It must be worked at, cultivated and constantly discussed and developed further. It needs clients who wish to go beyond mere building to create architecture. A substantial part of the Belgian production of architecture takes place on the small plot, which can be in the city, an agglomeration, or the urbanized countryside. The question of contemporary forms of living occupies clients and architects, and they use the freedom given them by society to arrive at innovative solutions in restricted spaces and with tight budgets. From a Swiss perspective this is precisely what makes Belgian architecture familiar and appealing: the culture of building there is neither characterized by loud gestures nor restricted to isolated 'grands projets' or to so-called 'beacon projects' in the major cities. Through everyday building commissions it percolates through to the small towns and villages, developing its impact precisely there where it is really needed. Part of this approach is that, like their Swiss colleagues, Belgian architects esteem and cultivate the handcrafted detail; wherever possible they themselves ensure that their buildings are well made – up to the handover of the keys. In this way they take on a responsibility that is part of a mature architectural culture.

THE QUALITIES OF BELGIAN ARCHITECTURE.

Caspar Schärer

Editor in chief | werk, bauen + wohnen

ENGLISH TRANSLATION: RODERICK O'DONOVAN

A GIANT STEP FORWARD.

Although a generation of architects has now emerged that feels not only Flemish or Walloon, but also international, European and perhaps even Belgian, writing about Belgian architecture is still more troublesome than writing about architecture in Belgium. For that matter, architecture in Belgium has recently taken a giant step forward. It is true that the starting point was not very high, but from that low point much progress has been made. This is even clearer in Flanders than in Wallonia, notably thanks to the Flemish Government Architect, the Open Calls and the rise of internationally leading designers. But in Wallonia, too, a little-known architectonic self-awareness has broken through, manifesting itself in a cultural and political activism that used to be a lot less tangible. It even seems that a – small – Brussels scene has developed, consisting of mostly young architects, for whom the language of architecture prevails, above and beyond the old linguistic divides.

Architectonic culture in Belgium is perhaps better off than ever, but it is the tragedy of this country that this frenzy should coincide with, and therefore in part be stifled by, the current economic stagnation.

Hans Ibelings
Editor in chief | The Architecture Observer
Former editor in chief | A10 new European architecture

THE ARCHITECTURE OF BELGIAN FAMILY HOMES ALWAYS MEETS WITH SURPRISE ABROAD.

Sebastian Redeke

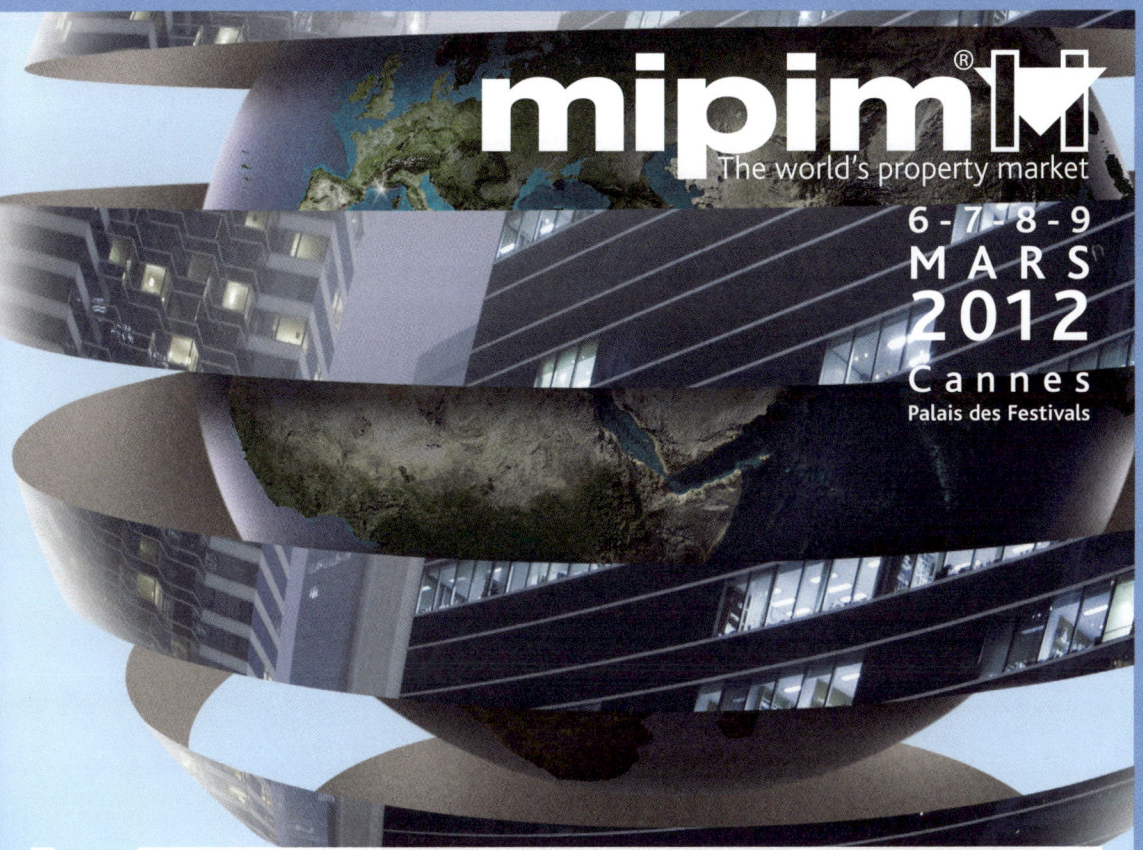

mipim® M
The world's property market

6 - 7 - 8 - 9
MARS
2012
Cannes
Palais des Festivals

INSCRIVEZ VOUS AVANT LE 21 FÉVRIER ET ÉCONOMISEZ 140€ !

▷ 4 jours pour participer à l'évènement clé de l'industrie immobilier
▷ 18 000 participants uniques
▷ 4 000 investisseurs
▷ 1 800 sociétés exposantes
▷ 90 pays
▷ 1 pays à l'honneur en 2012 : Allemagne

Venez découvrir les projets les plus prometteurs, des partenaires influents, acquérir de l'information pointue sur l'industrie, rencontrer les acteurs internationaux incontournables du monde de l'immobilier au MIPIM 2012.

BUILDING GLOBAL OPPORTUNITIES*

*Construisez vos opportunités

KOBLENZ BELVEDERE
KOBLENZ | GERMANY
DETHIER ARCHITECTURES

TEXT Gilles Béchet
PHOTOGRAPHY Thomas Faes – Dethier Architectures

Woodwork, and more particularly the construction of
viewing platforms and belvederes, is one of the facets of
Daniel Dethier's work. This is what drove the organizers
of the Federal Horticultural Show held in Koblenz in 2011 to
include his name on the select list of architects invited to
submit a project for the design of a viewing platform. On
the occasion of this two-yearly horticultural show, the city
on the Rhine had undertaken a vast urban redevelopment
programme. The organizers wished to set up a wooden
observation platform at the centre of a park redesigned by
an Austrian firm. This platform would act as a promenade
while offering panoramic views of the city and its two rivers.
The model submitted for the competition by Daniel Dethier
consisted of a triangle with sides measuring 30 metres,
set down like a triangle clip on the landscape. Each of
its sides offers two promenade levels with a five-percent
slope. "I wanted to create an enjoyable space where people
could observe and wave to one another", Dethier explains.
Although the lines of the platform are simple, its geometry
is complex: there are some 100 different joints, and the floor
is separated from the main structure. The project, one of
Dethier's first in Germany, faced several unforeseen hurdles.
In order to be awarded the contract, for instance, Dethier
had to join the Federal Chamber of German Architects.
And construction was delayed by a few weeks due to a
misunderstanding surrounding the Eurocode standards
used by the engineer Laurent Ney, and which are recognized throughout Europe, and those used by the German
engineer to recalculate the drawings. The project manager's
trust and support made it possible to identify and solve the
problem. "Since we had been called on for our specific skills,
we had the backing of an expert, which made the work
easier". Throughout the horticultural show, the viewing
platform, which was designed to last for 30 years with no
need for maintenance work, was the second most visited
attraction, drawing over two million visitors. "The people
have appropriated this space, and it is now part of the
city's identity. This is one of the reasons why I became an
architect", Daniel Dethier is happy to say.

Daniel Dethier is the architect behind the wooden viewing platform in the park beneath the fortress of Koblenz. Construction on this simple-looking yet geometrically complex structure hit several hurdles, which were overcome with the support of the project manager.

KOBLENZ BELVEDERE
KOBLENZ | GERMANY
DETHIER ARCHITECTURES

ALTHOUGH THE LINES OF THE PLATFORM
ARE SIMPLE, ITS GEOMETRY IS COMPLEX:
THERE ARE SOME 100 DIFFERENT JOINTS,
AND THE FLOOR IS SEPARATED FROM
THE MAIN STRUCTURE.

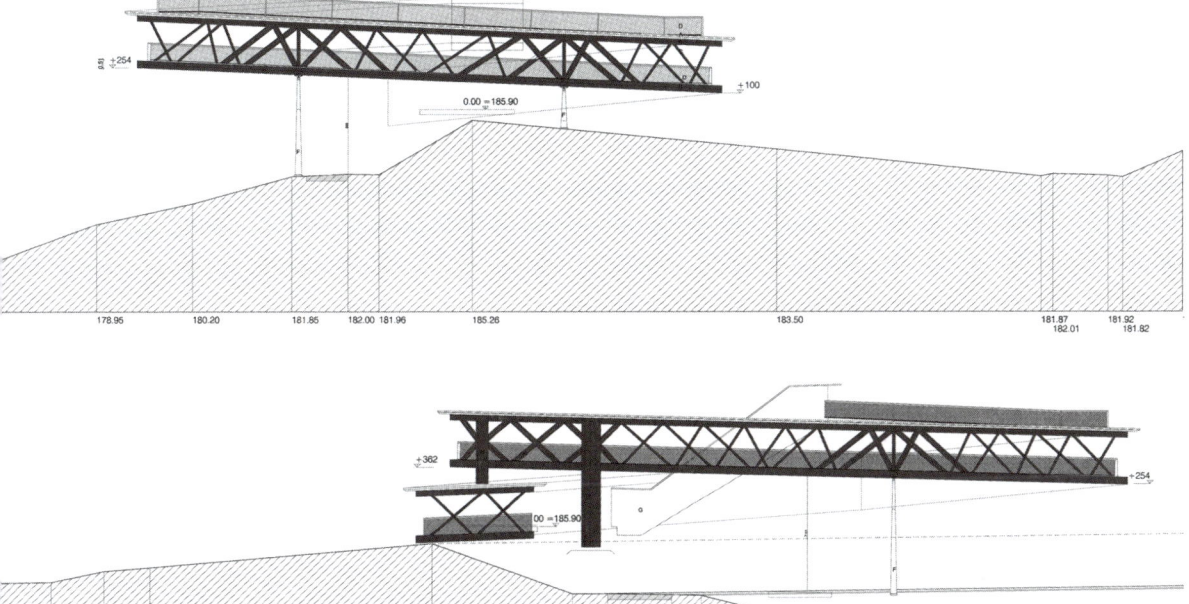

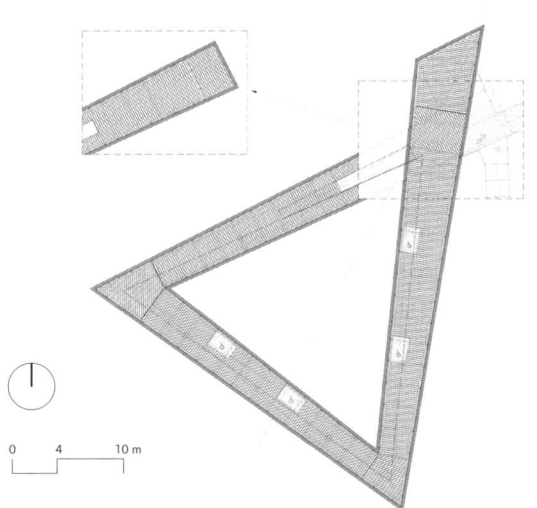

0   4   10 m

Koblenz belvedere

PROGRAMME construction of a wooden belvedere
ARCHITECT Dethier Architectures
CLIENT Bundesgartenschau Koblenz 2011
STABILITY Ney & Partners CARPENTRY Mohr Ingenieurholzbau
AREA 675 m² BUDGET (excluding VAT and fees) 450 000 euro
COMPLETED May 2011
www.dethier.be

MILLAU VIADUCT
TARN VALLEY | FRANCE
BUREAU GREISCH

TEXT Gilles Béchet
PHOTOGRAPHY Jean-Luc Deru

For several decades, art publications have been offering an international showcase to the engineering firm Bureau Greisch, even though this activity represents only 15% of their revenue. Bridges and viaducts stand out through their shape and building method, but also their reliance on soaring metallic structures. "Belgian engineers have a very good knowledge of the behaviour of these structures. Given the region's steel-producing past, the University of Liège has always been at the forefront of research and training in these techniques", says Vincent de Ville de Goyet, one of the firm's directors. Bureau Greisch has always sought to use innovative building methods, notably privileging on-the-ground assembly to improve security and thus work efficiency. In France, where the use of cement is predominant in the public works sector, much interest has been shown for the expertise of the Liège-based team in the field of metallic structures. First called on as an engineering consultancy for road works (Lille, Toulouse, etc.), Bureau Greisch was later invited to take charge of the study and proportioning of viaducts for the French high-speed train (Haute-Colme, Aix-en-Provence, Mornas, Mondragon, Donzère). The reputation of the firm's expertise grew, and initial contacts were established with developers such as Eiffel. In late 1999, the French authorities launched a competition for the Millau Viaduct, which would measure 2460 metres and span the Tarn valley. Little known at the time, the Eiffage group proposed two projects: the first consisted entirely of cement, and the second of metallic pylons and a metallic deck. For the latter, Greisch joined forces with Eiffel, that had become Eiffage Construction Métallique. "Many people believed that cement was the only possible option. They were amazed by the building method we put forward". By assembling segments of the steel deck on the ground before gradually moving them into their final position, it was possible to conduct 95% of the work in optimal security conditions, as was confirmed by the fact that there was only one accident to deplore: a broken foot. Construction lasted 38 months, and throughout this time Bureau Greisch's engineers were able to rely on the advice given by professors of the University of Liège, with whom they had created specific modelling tools to examine the impact of wind on the structure, but also to reassure their French associates who, with some concern, watched the sheets of steel bend like gum during the assembly process. The technological feat of the Millau project did not go unnoticed in the sector, ensuring other orders for Bureau Greisch, including the new stadium in Lille and the (currently on hold) Louis Vuitton Foundation for Creation in Paris, designed by Frank Gehry. However, this has not prevented the firm from continuing to take part in competitions, in France and elsewhere. "Even though it can pay poorly in relation to the amount of work involved, it is indispensable if we want to show ourselves. If we want to obtain a project, we cannot afford to submit something sketched out rapidly on the corner of a table, since the price given by the firm will depend on the precision of the study in terms of design quality and the estimated quantity of material". In less than 20 years, the engineering firm Bureau Greisch has more than tripled its personnel, which currently totals some 175 staff members, proof of its expertise and the guarantee of future challenges.

Although Bureau Greisch is a little known name outside the profession, its work on the design and construction of the Millau Viaduct is a reference in its sector, proof of the expertise and innovative approach of the Liège-based engineering firm in the field of metallic structures.

MILLAU VIADUCT
TARN VALLEY | FRANCE
BUREAU GREISCH

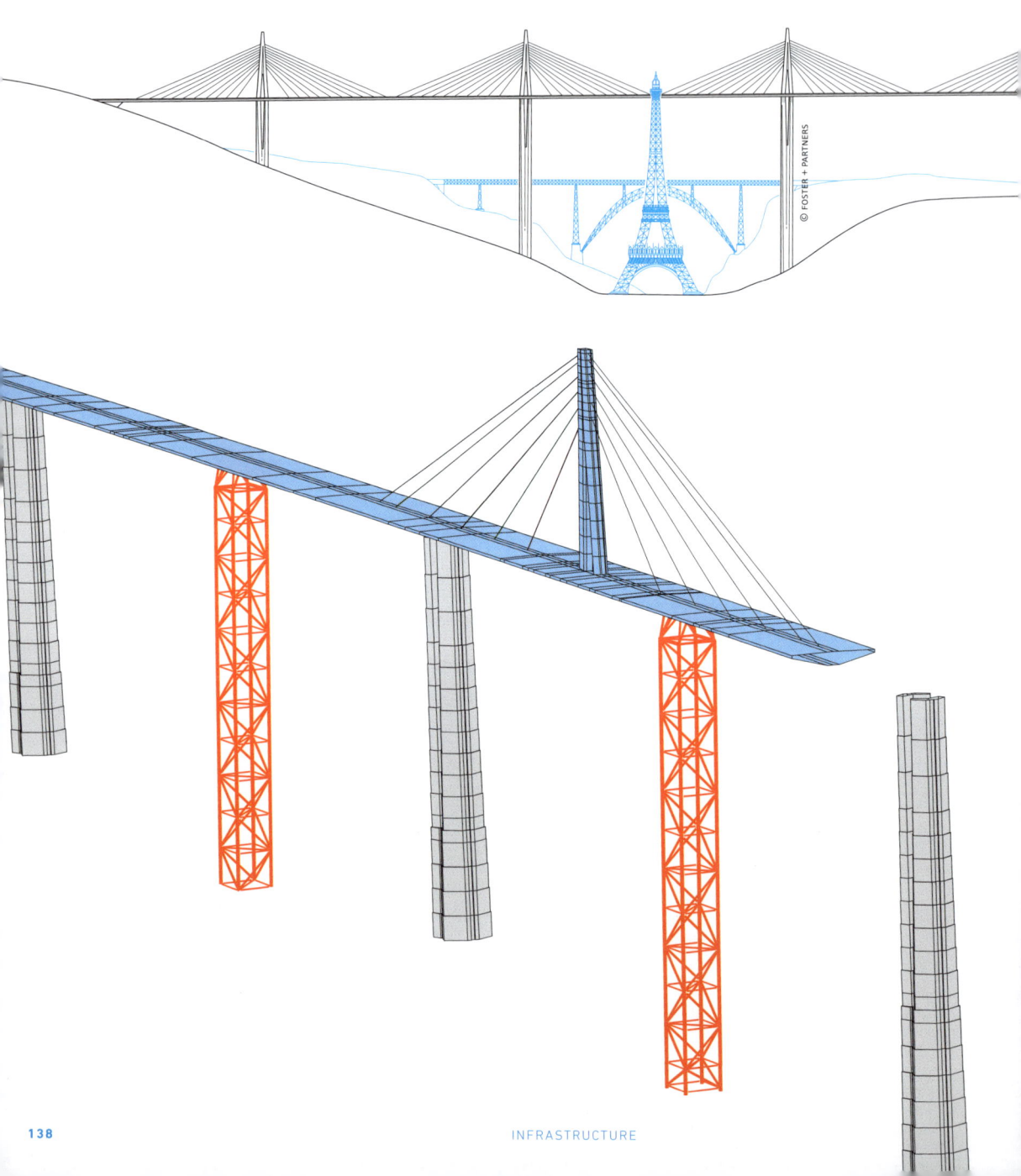

© FOSTER + PARTNERS

THE TECHNOLOGICAL FEAT OF THE MILLAU
PROJECT DID NOT GO UNNOTICED IN THE
SECTOR, ENSURING OTHER ORDERS FOR
BUREAU GREISCH, INCLUDING THE NEW
STADIUM IN LILLE.

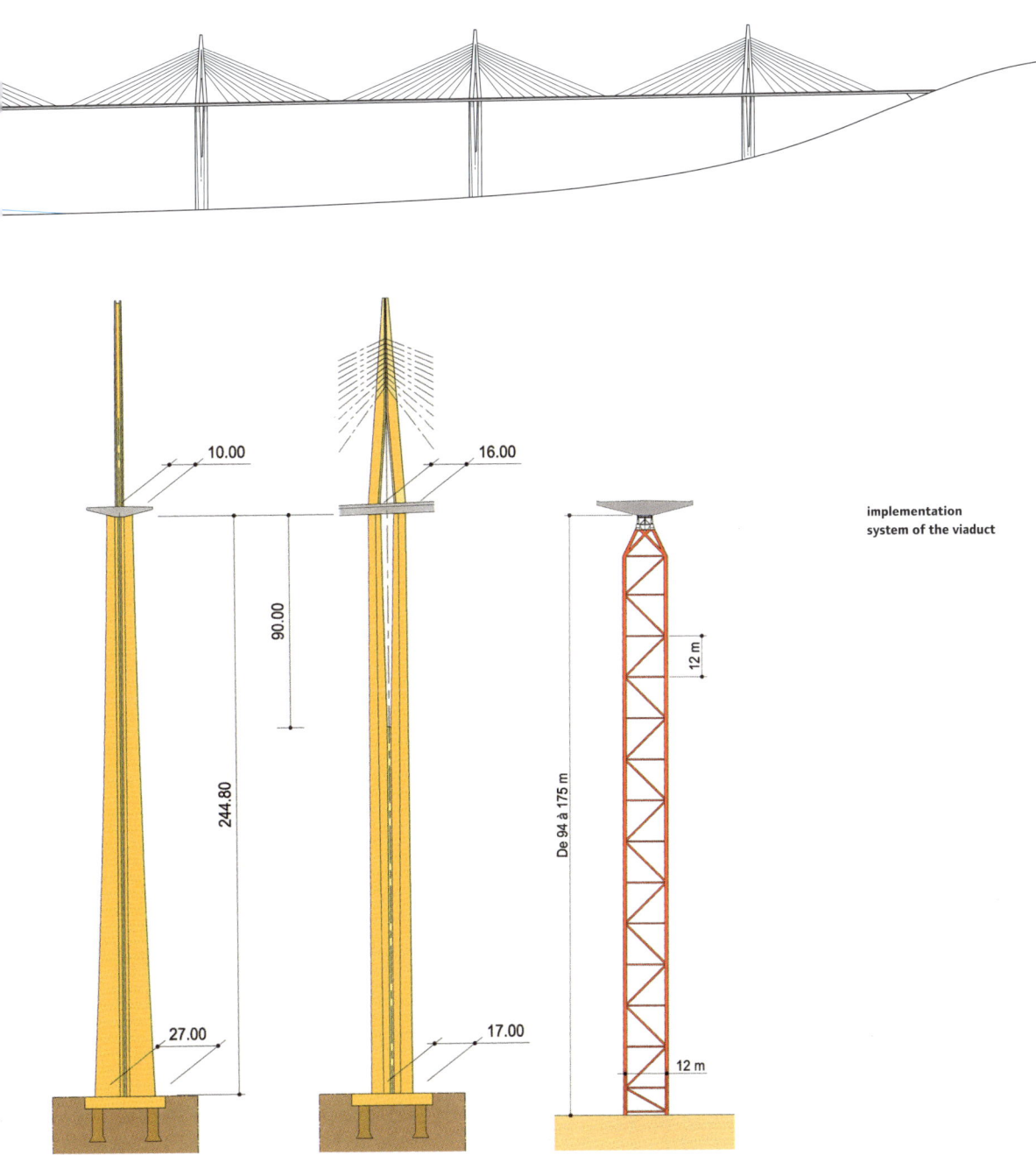

implementation
system of the viaduct

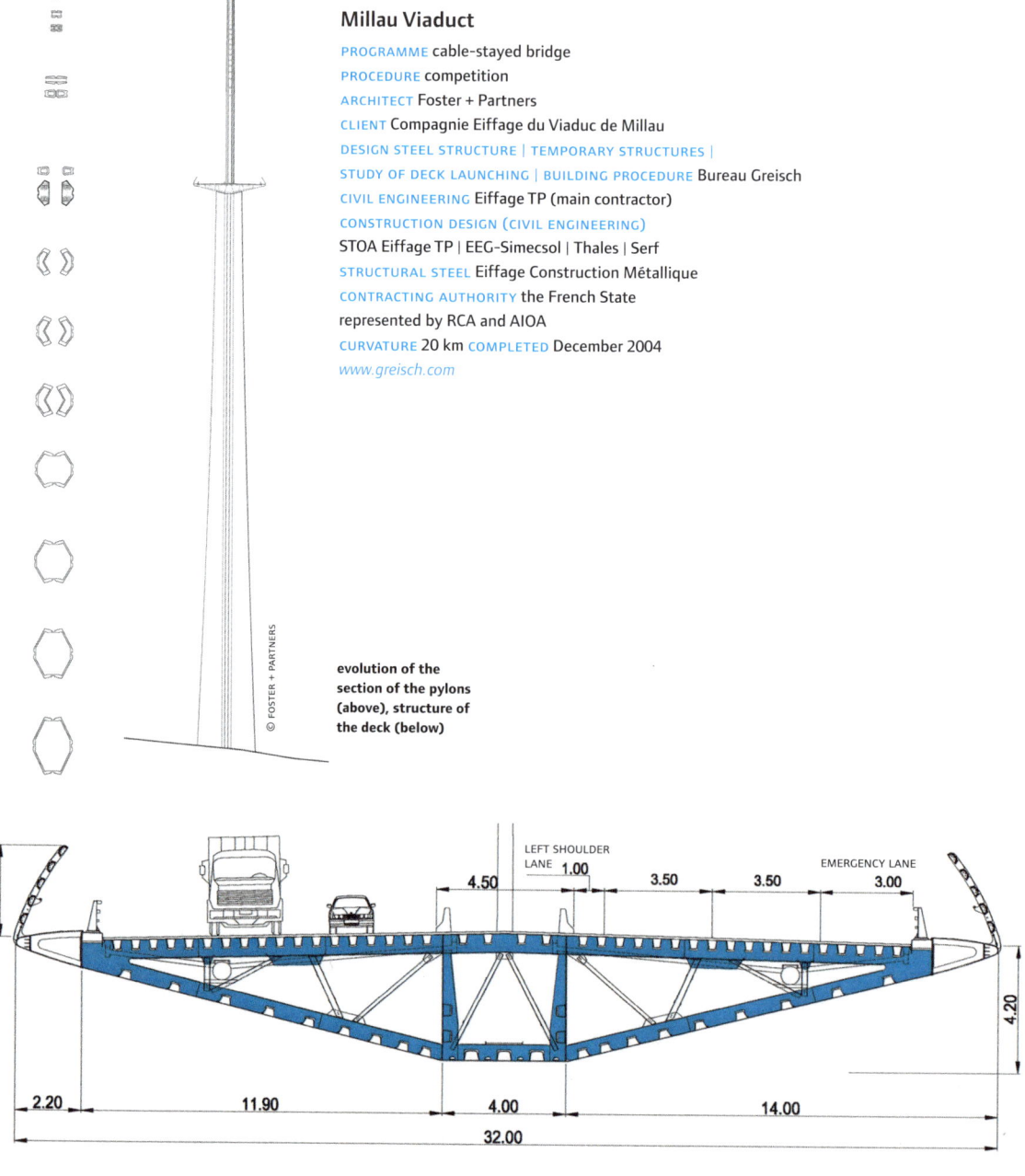

Millau Viaduct

PROGRAMME cable-stayed bridge
PROCEDURE competition
ARCHITECT Foster + Partners
CLIENT Compagnie Eiffage du Viaduc de Millau
DESIGN STEEL STRUCTURE | TEMPORARY STRUCTURES |
STUDY OF DECK LAUNCHING | BUILDING PROCEDURE Bureau Greisch
CIVIL ENGINEERING Eiffage TP (main contractor)
CONSTRUCTION DESIGN (CIVIL ENGINEERING)
STOA Eiffage TP | EEG-Simecsol | Thales | Serf
STRUCTURAL STEEL Eiffage Construction Métallique
CONTRACTING AUTHORITY the French State
represented by RCA and AIOA
CURVATURE 20 km COMPLETED December 2004
www.greisch.com

© FOSTER + PARTNERS

**evolution of the
section of the pylons
(above), structure of
the deck (below)**

3.00

LEFT SHOULDER
LANE 1.00
4.50   3.50   3.50   EMERGENCY LANE
                                    3.00

4.20

2.20   11.90   4.00   14.00

32.00

awg architecten, gebouw Detroit in Amsterdam

DO YOU HAVE PLANS
FOR A PROJECT
ABROAD?
WE CAN HELP.

As a Flemish architect, are you looking to do work abroad? If so, then Flanders Investment &
Trade (FIT) can offer you their support in many ways. By providing a host of contacts. And by
searching all useful information about subsidies, laws and customs issues you will need.

Don't hesitate to take contact with Flanders Investment & Trade. We can help you build your
reputation abroad.

www.flanderstrade.be

HOLMENKOLLEN SKI JUMP
OSLO | NORWAY
JDS ARCHITECTS

TEXT Cécile Vandernoot
PHOTOGRAPHY Felix Luong

"I think it is just as interesting to build next door to home as it is on the other side of the planet", begins Julien De Smedt, the director and founder of the architectural firm JDS Architects. This Belgian architect with an uncommon curriculum is a tireless traveller, who has seized the opportunities that presented themselves to him and this, ever since his college years (six schools in six years). After a fruitful passage in Copenhagen, where he founded PLOT with the Danish architect Bjarke Ingels, he returned to Brussels in 2006. Armed with projects in Scandinavia totalling some 100 000 m², he hoped to give a boost to the emerging Brussels scene.

By returning to his sources, Julien De Smedt was eager to put his experience at the service of the city, and he confesses that he was hoping for a warmer welcome. "Only one local project – a police station in Antwerp that can be converted into a housing complex in a few years – is currently under construction. The rest is scattered around the world; commissions are mostly obtained through an international social and professional network or through competitions. It is the immediacy of the connections between people that creates the work abroad; it is ubiquitous in this global society made up of exchanges". Most recently, for instance, JDS was commissioned to fit out a 40 000 m² warehouse in New York for the Brooklyn Night Bazaar: this three-night event gathered local artisans and craft vendors of all kinds, and featured concerts and DJ sets. The project was obtained through a network of acquaintances in the New York arts scene and was completed in record time. The layout of the warehouse, something like an urban-development master plan scaled to the size of the building, was far from the programmes usually managed by the firm, notably in terms of size. The Hedonistic Rooftop Penthouses inaugurated last year is a renovation project in the Elmegade district of Copenhagen, whose building density resembles that of downtown Brussels. Following the principle of the roof terrace, JDS redesigned the top floor with its set-back mansard roof. Three penthouses were created, and the new roof provided ample common space for the residents. The garden-terrace, which fills the entire plot, overlooks the neighbourhood, and was positively received by all co-owners. "Working on a range of different-sized projects in distinct contexts, increasing the number of geographical locations, projects and collaborations has always been important", explains Julien De Smedt. "It is part of our architectural approach: to develop several proposals in order to arrive at a single solution that will meet all the relevant criteria". The firm now has several branches, in Copenhagen, Shanghai and, most recently, Belo Horizonte, in Brazil. "We keep exporting our services. When I am on the move, the teams working on the different projects send me a daily PDF file on the state of progress and we communicate through video-conferencing. The advantage to long-distance travel is that it provides precious moments for reflection". Working abroad has become a way of thinking.

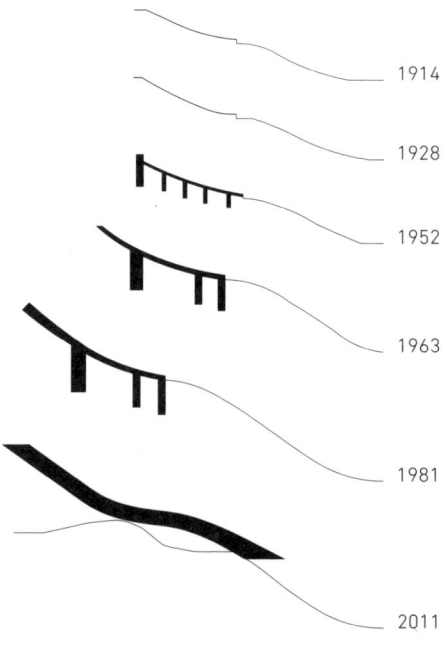

1914

1928

1952

1963

1981

2011

Although most of its activity is focused elsewhere, JDS Architects recently moved into new offices in Brussels. Work abroad represents the fruit of a series of international commissions, but is also – regrettably – a necessity, given the few local commissions.

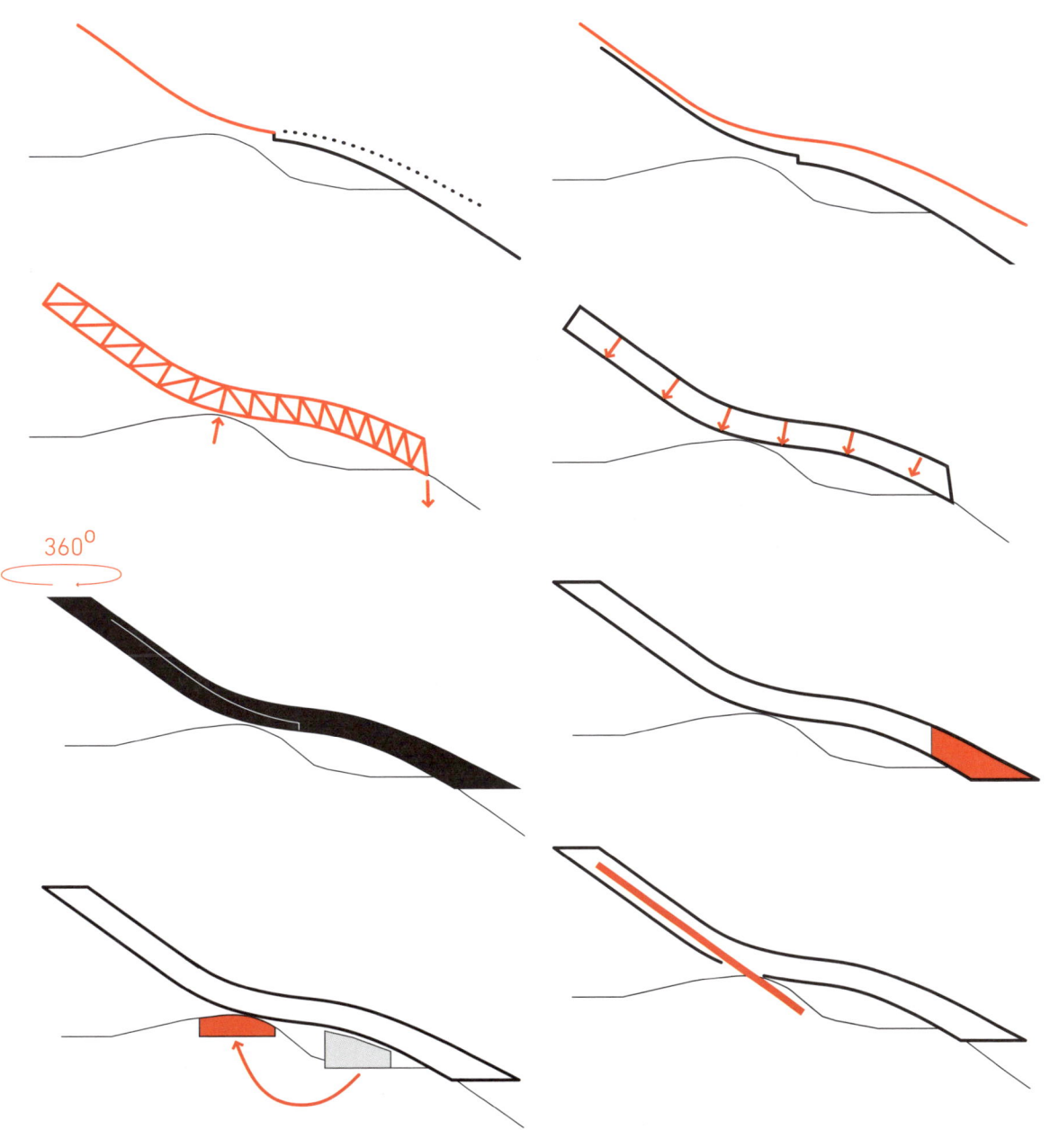

OSLO

HOLMENKOLLEN SKI JUMP
OSLO | NORWAY
JDS ARCHITECTS

I THINK IT IS JUST AS INTERESTING TO BUILD
NEXT DOOR TO HOME AS IT IS ON THE OTHER
SIDE OF THE PLANET.

Holmenkollen ski jump

PROGRAMME ski jump, large jumping hill and
touristdestination with viewing plateau, souvenir shop,
café and corresponding museum
PROCEDURE open competition ARCHITECT JDS Architects
CLIENT the City of Oslo, Idrettsetaten
STRUCTURAL WORK Norconsult LANDSCAPE Grindaker
FAÇADE AND STEEL DETAILS Metallplan
GROUND WORK | CONCRETE Veidekke
STEEL CONSTRUCTIONS | FAÇADE | IN-RUN | WINDSCREEN Lecor
JUMP TECHNICAL IBM | Ivar Bråten Mekaniske
BUDGET 87 300 000 euro
COMPLETED February 2011
www.jdsa.eu

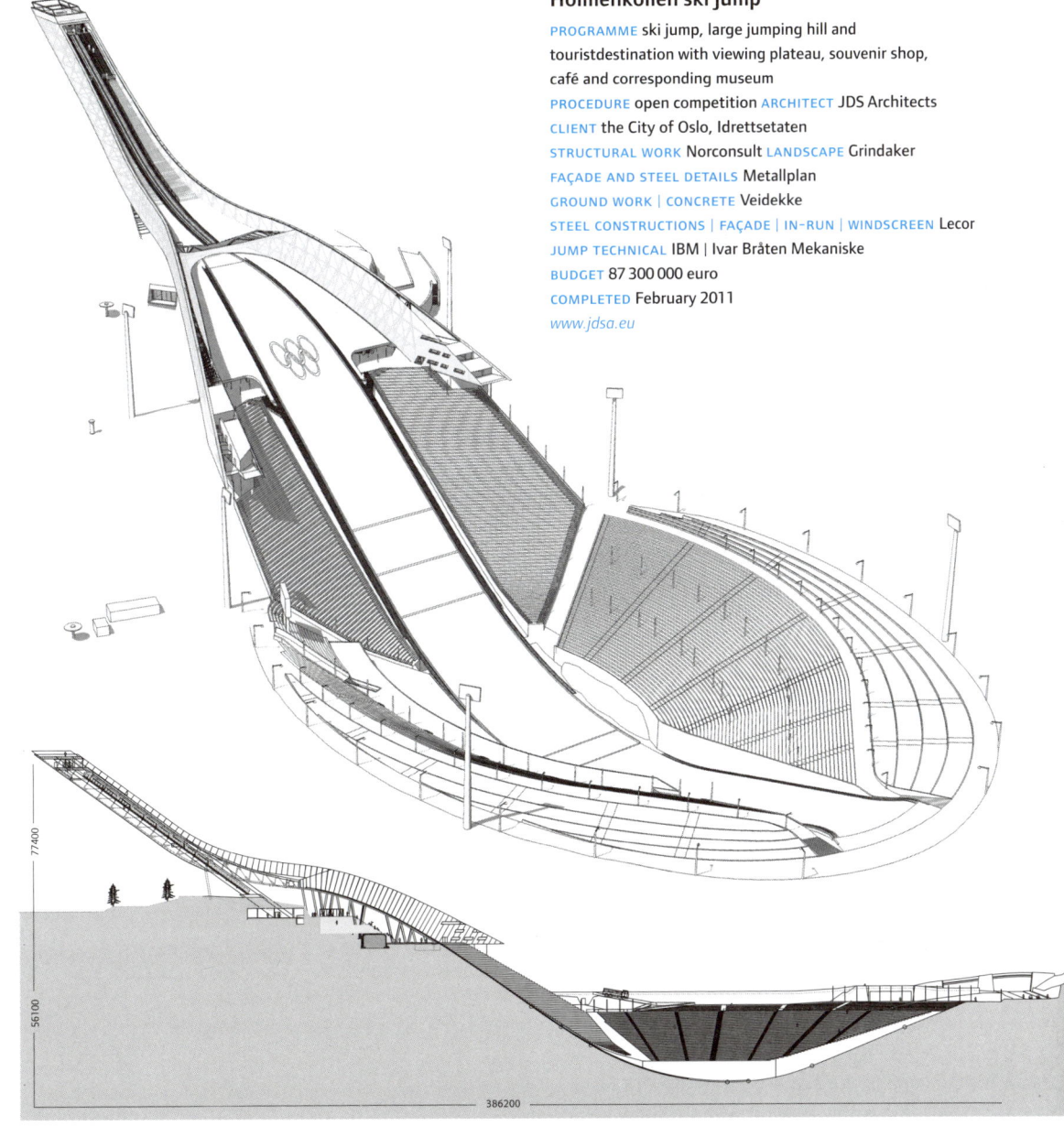

77400

56100

386200

TEXT Gilles Béchet

An area of 1200 m² with no support. And when night falls, the vault is lit up with countless little lights. The glass roof conceived by Laurent Ney to cover the courtyard of the National Maritime Museum in Amsterdam is both a technical feat and a work of the imagination. It all started with a competition by invitation which the Belgian engineer won, beating two other projects, including one submitted by the renowned German engineer Jörg Schleich. It was a complex mission. In no way could the building, a former warehouse of the Dutch military fleet dating from the 17th century, be disfigured. "One of the things that drove them to choose us is that we were the only ones to propose a project without any supporting structures in the courtyard", observes Eric Bodarwé, an associate and the project engineer. The client also appreciated the complete harmony between the structure and the building's symbolism. During its golden age, the Dutch navy ruled the waves, and the large square building was thus a metaphor for the centre of the world. When developing the project, Laurent Ney drew inspiration from old nautical maps and the navigation charts that are traced on them. The result is a complex metal structure reproducing an enlarged rose-window motif to create a network comprising no less than 800 points of intersection. Each of these points is fitted with an led lamp that can be controlled individually. The work was executed by the Antwerp-based company Anmeco, which won the call for tenders and had already been recommended by Ney & Partners. The structure was assembled on site, welded on a scaffold, and then moved into position. "We didn't encounter any particular technical problems, except that, because of their complex shape, the glass panes had to be tailored individually, one by one". Due to the symbolic and historical value of the building, the Dutch heritage and monument officials were very reserved until the end, and it is only once the work was completed that they were convinced they had made the right choice. For Ney & Partners, the feedback was impressive. The project was much talked about in

the Netherlands. It was the firm's first large-scale project abroad, and it has enabled them to make a lot of interesting connections. Between the launch of the competition and the inauguration of the building, seven years went by. "It is a very long process for a return on investment, but it is important to be able to stand out thanks to a reference abroad such as this", concludes Eric Bodarwé.

The glass roof covering the courtyard of the National
Maritime Museum in Amsterdam was conceived
by Ney & Partners. The original design of this
technically daring project blended perfectly with
this listed building.

© JEAN-LUC DERU

GLASS ROOF OF MARITIME MUSEUM COURTYARD
NATIONAL MARITIME MUSEUM | NETHERLANDS
NEY & PARTNERS

© BRS BUILDING SYSTEMS BV

NEY & PARTNERS

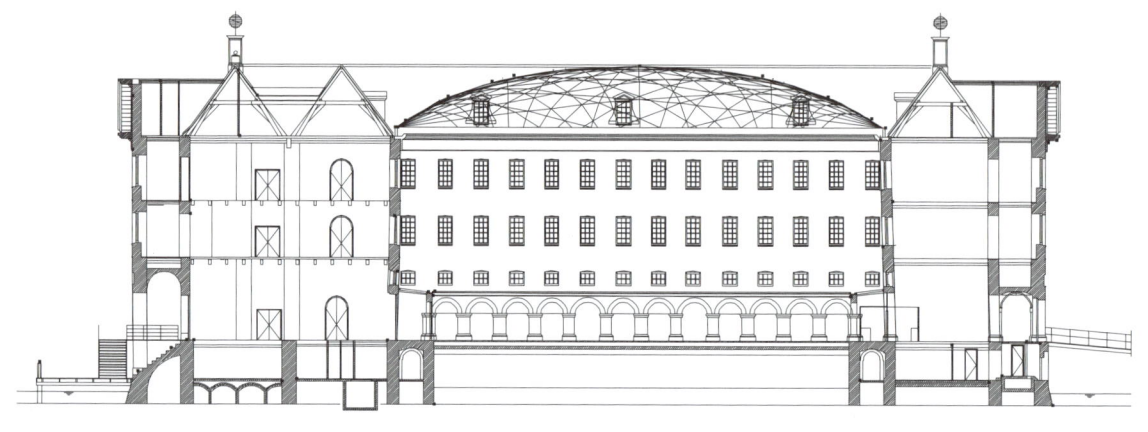

© MARTIN WAALBOER

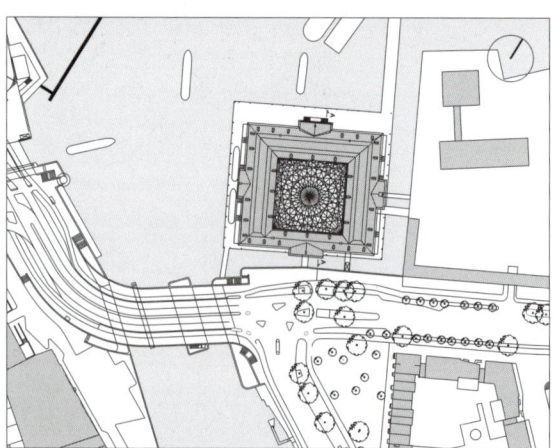

Glass roof of National Maritime Museum courtyard

PROGRAMME steel roof structure with glass

PROCEDURE competition, later European tender

ARCHITECT Ney & Partners

CLIENT Rijksgebouwendienst Haarlem

STABILITY Ney & Partners ACOUSTICS LBP | SIGHT

EXECUTION (metal structure) Anmeco

GLAZING BRS Building Systems SURFACE 1000 m²

BUDGET (excluding VAT and fees) 3 200 000 euro

COMPLETED May 2011

www.ney.be | www.hetscheepvaartmuseum.nl

BRUSSELS
invest & export
Building new perspectives

CONSTRUCTION IS ONE OF THE KEY ECONOMIC SECTORS IN BRUSSELS !

Public organisations and private companies are investing time, money and efforts on a daily basis in order to develop together a region that combines a multitude of styles that go way back: from medieval town walls to gothic churches, from classic brick buildings to modern business offices, from Art Nouveau to Art Deco to square structures.

Brussels counts numerous ongoing construction projects that are being realized with the help of Brussels' designers, architects, engineers, construction companies, traders and producers of equipment and/or materials. Some of these companies are equally active, and even renowned, in foreign markets.

In order to support and promote these companies, Brussels Invest & Export has decided to organise in 2012 a Brussels pavilion at MIPIM in Cannes, at Mosbuild in Russia, Project Qatar in Doha and finally at Realty in Brussels all this with the support of the government of the Brussels-Capital Region.

Brussels Invest & Export has recently created a website dedicated to Brussels based architects that have achieved projects on foreign markets and wish to develop their experience abroad.

You can consult their profiles on **architectes.mypublisher.be.**

MINISTRY OF THE BRUSSELS-CAPITAL REGION

ORIGINAL PHOTO © 354 PHOTOGRAPHERS

ZAC SÉGUIN RIVES DE SEINE | MACROLOT B2
BOULOGNE-BILLANCOURT (PARIS) | FRANCE
STEPHANE BEEL ARCHITECTS | UAPS

TEXT Christophe Van Gerrewey
PHOTOGRAPHY Luca Beel

Over the last decade, the former site of the Renault factories in Boulogne-Billancourt has been transformed into an entirely new area. 'La Rive de Billancourt' was inaugurated in October 2009. By means of the Renault bridge, the area is accessible from the Seguin island, on the right bank of the Seine, to the west of the Parisian metropolitan region.

French architect Patrick Chavannes and landscape designer Thierry Laverne were asked by the public-private partnership SAEM Val de Seine Aménagement to develop the site. The development consists of housing (50%), offices (25%) and cultural venues (25%), and it includes a spacious public area. Chavannes and Laverne commissioned a plethora of architects of international renown such as Dominique Perrault, Jean Nouvel, Norman Foster, Josep Lluis Mateo, Jakob & MacFarlane, and KCAP. For the urban design of Macrolot B2, a subdivision of the site consisting of 35 000 m² of private and social housing, offices, shops and a school, they organized a competition that was only accessible by invitation. It was won by Stéphane Beel Architects, working closely with the Paris-based office uapS (led by the Belgian architects Anne Mie Depuydt and Erik Van Daele), and the Paris-Brussels office for landscape and urbanism Taktyk.

Sebastiaan Leenknegt has written on their design in a monograph dedicated to the work of Stéphane Beel Architects and entitled New Works & Words, published in 2011 by Lannoo. "The design team divided the plot into four zones, each of which was to be developed as a specific type of semi-public space. The 'jardin en pente' is a garden leaning towards the office building, thereby exposing the subterranean level. The 'cours' consist of a number of play areas for the school, dispersed across several levels. The 'jardin sous bois' is a terraced tree garden. And the 'place', finally, is comprised of a kind of sculpted plaza, intersected by some lines of greenery. Each of these elements connects with a specific part of the programme. The whole layout is intersected by a north-south and an east-west circulation axis. (…)

The structure of the new master plan subscribes to the principles underlying many other Parisian 'ilots' – but by its division into four zones it at once attributes a fresh, qualified meaning to the notion of semi-private spaces within a block".

The buildings on the site were all designed individually – within the limits imposed by the master plan – by Stéphane Beel Architects, uapS, Carlos Ferrater, Clément Vergely and Gaëlte Peneau. Writing on Beel's apartment block, Leenknegt wrote that "even more so than the master plan, [it] refuses to make unequivocal statements. Yet its seemingly plain appearance is merely a pretence, for the silence is far from boring; it is laden with anticipation, like the silence in a packed theatre just before the start of a performance".

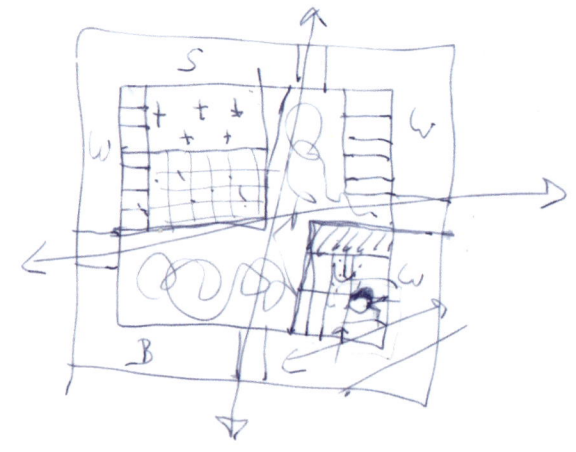

Over the last decade, the former site of the Renault factories in Boulogne-Billancourt has been transformed into an entirely new area. 'La Rive de Billancourt' was inaugurated in October 2009.

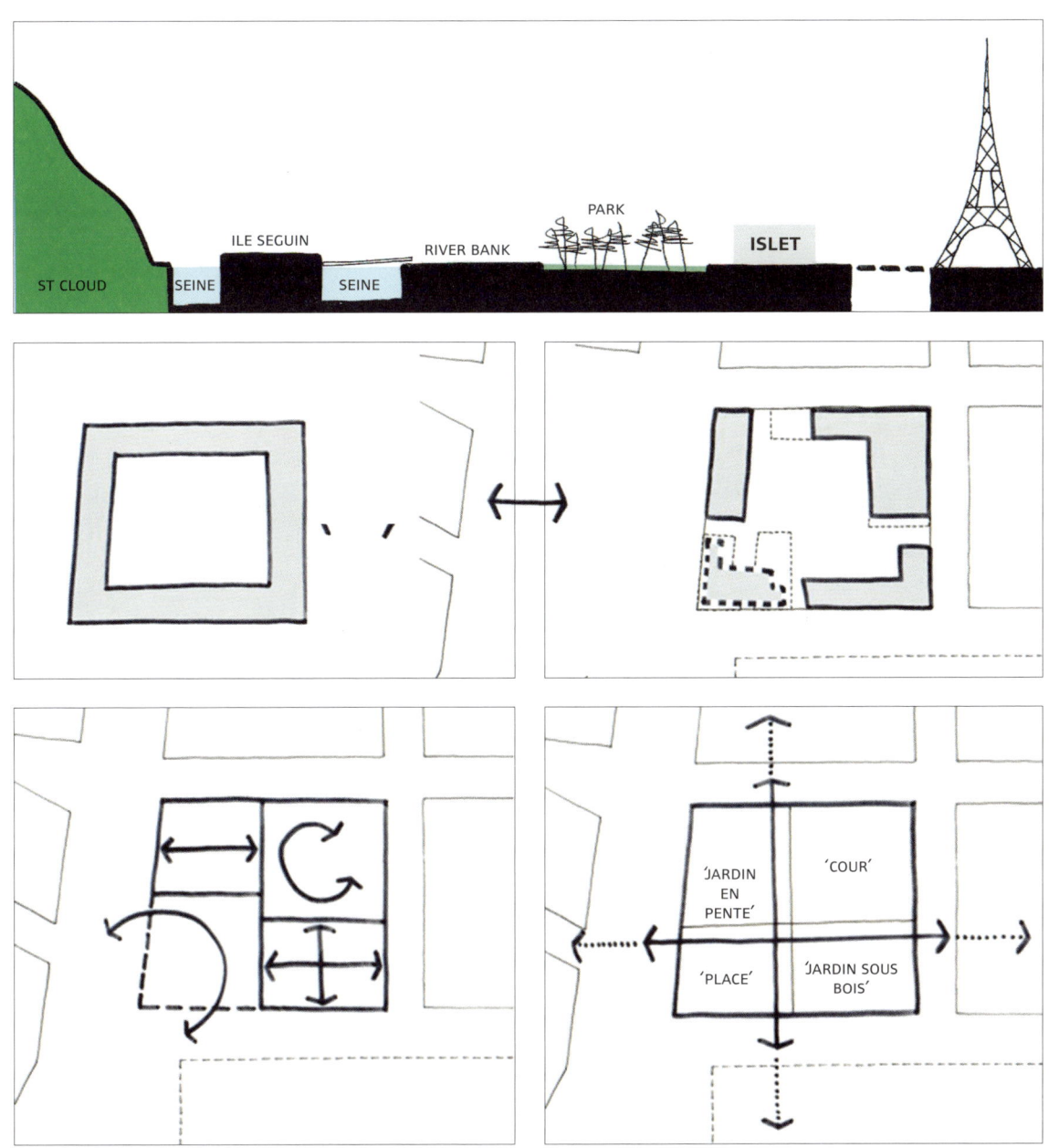

ZAC SÉGUIN – RIVES DE SEINE | MACROLOT B2
BOULOGNE-BILLANCOURT (PARIS) | FRANCE
STEPHANE BEEL ARCHITECTS | UAPS

© STÉPHANE BEEL ARCHITECTEN

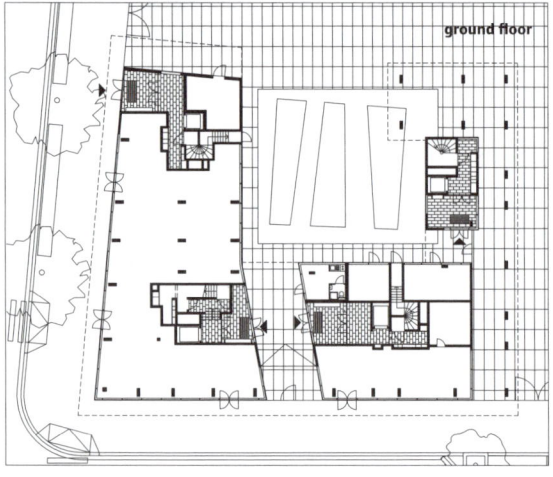

ground floor

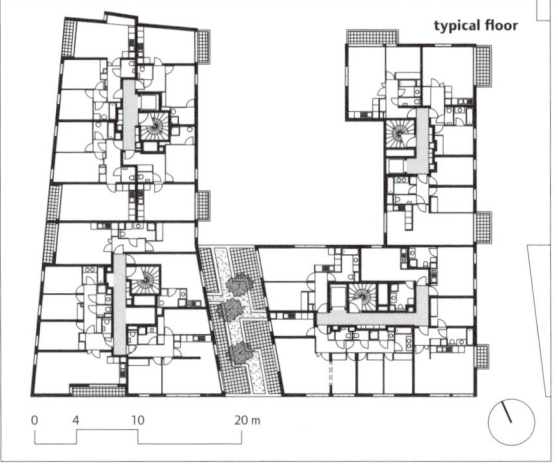

typical floor

0   4   10   20 m

ITS SEEMINGLY PLAIN APPEARANCE IS MERELY
A PRETENCE, FOR THE SILENCE IS FAR FROM
BORING; IT IS LADEN WITH ANTICIPATION, LIKE
THE SILENCE IN A PACKED THEATRE JUST
BEFORE THE START OF A PERFORMANCE.

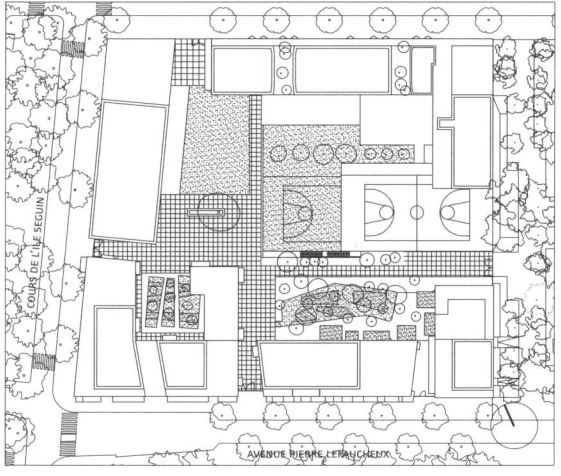

Zac Séguin – Rives de Seine, macrolot B2

PROGRAMME urban development plan macrolot B2 with apartments,
commercial spaces and underground car park
PROCEDURE competition (first application, later selection)
ARCHITECT Stéphane Beel Architects | UAPS
CLIENT SCI Boulogne Parc B2 (Nexity Foncière Colysée | Icade Promotion
Logement) LANDSCAPE ARCHITECT Taktyk landscape + urbanism
STABILITY | TECHNIQUES | ACOUSTICS CET Ingénierie
STRUCTURAL WORK | WORKMANSHIP OF INTERIOR Eiffage Construction
CARPENTRY Seraba menuiserie ELECTRICITY SCIE
HEATING UTB AREA macrolot 35 000 m² | 116 apartments 7390 m² |
commercial spaces 394 m² | underground car park 9750 m²
BUDGET (excluding VAT and fees) 14 100 000 euro
COMPLETED October 2010
www.stephanebeel.com

CREPAIN BINST ARCHITECTURE

TEXT Gilles Béchet
PHOTOGRAPHY Crepain Binst Architecture

It was a real challenge. The Dutch commune of Goirle
near Tilburg launched a competition for the creation of
a housing complex in a wooded area running along the
A58 motorway. The architectural firm Crepain Binst, in
association with the Dutch landscape architecture firm
Buro Lubbers, stood out among four other candidates.
The 178 housing units are built against a wall measuring
14 metres in height and 750 metres in length, which cuts
across the landscape like a knife. The high wall separating
the residences from the flow of cars is covered with rows
of bricks in five shades of grey and is pierced with narrow
horizontal windows similar to the arrow slits of a medieval
fortress. The south-facing side, turned towards the woods,
offers a striking contrast due to the succession of open
volumes of varying widths and heights. The Belgian
project was chosen for its sculptural and acoustic qualities,
since the wall was designed to isolate the dwellings as
much as possible from the noise of the traffic.

Present in the Netherlands since 1989, Crepain Binst has
built many housing complexes there. "Their work method
is quite different from the one we practise in Belgium.
Architects have to be efficient and productive. Prefab
elements are a lot more common, although the completion is not always as meticulous", explains Luc Binst.
Since the 1950s, the Dutch authorities have conducted an
intensive housing construction policy and the demand
is still high, thus driving the authorities to make use of
unexpected lots, like the one in Goirle. "Housing units are
generally smaller and more diversified, which drives the
architect to suggest new solutions".

Over the last two years, the building market in the
Netherlands has suffered a marked decline. Crepain Binst
has fallen back on Belgium, and was followed by many
Dutch firms, which have taken a more aggressive commercial approach to the Belgian market.

Luc Binst sees this competition as a challenge. "By
combining Belgian know-how with the efficiency we
developed in the Netherlands, we feel well equipped to
target other markets in Europe and even in Asia".

Crepain Binst is behind a housing complex in the Netherlands that was built on a narrow strip of land next to a motorway. Not only was the acoustic challenge taken up successfully, but the project was also lauded for its typomorphological and spatial qualities.

HOUSING COMPLEX
GOIRLE | NETHERLANDS
CREPAIN BINST ARCHITECTURE

section 1 (apartments)

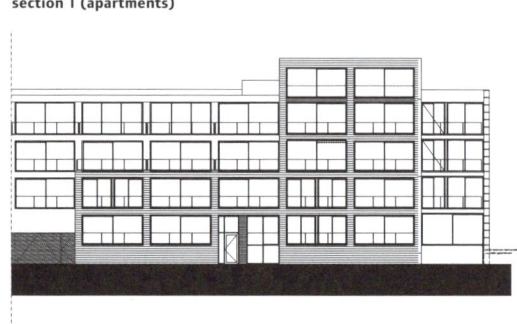

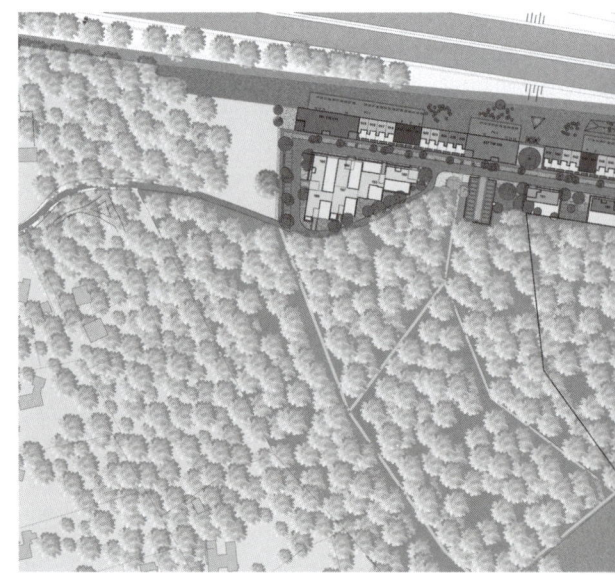

THE BELGIAN PROJECT WAS CHOSEN FOR ITS
SCULPTURAL AND ACOUSTIC QUALITIES, SINCE
THE WALL WAS DESIGNED TO ISOLATE THE
DWELLINGS AS MUCH AS POSSIBLE FROM THE
NOISE OF THE TRAFFIC.

section 2 (apartments)

sections (villas)

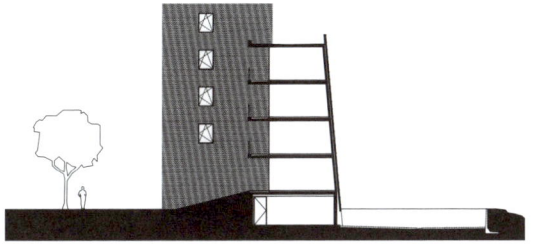

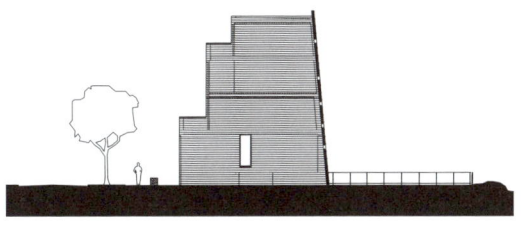

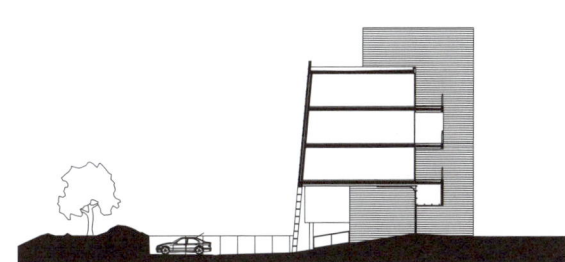

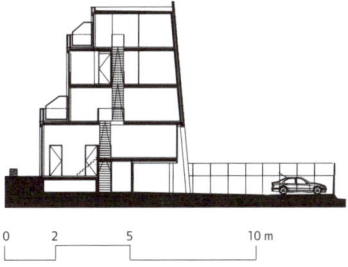

0   2   5   10 m

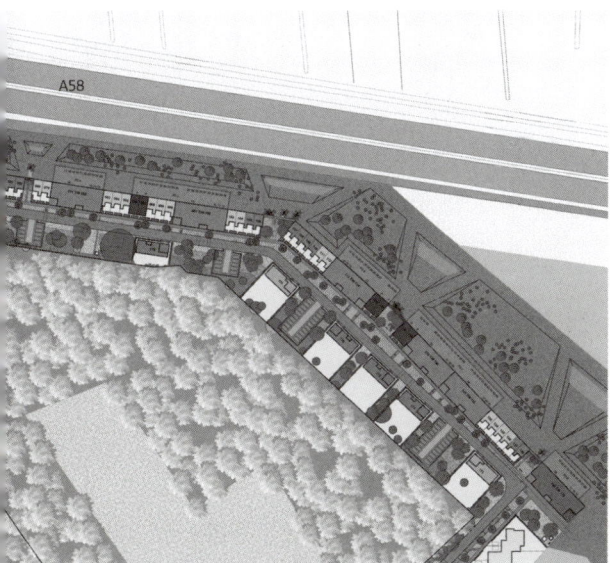

A58

Boschkens Goirle housing complex

PROGRAMME 112 apartments and 66 single
family houses along a noise barrier on the A58
motorway PROCEDURE competition
ARCHITECT Crepain Binst Architecture
CLIENT Bouwfonds Ontwikkeling Regio Zuid
LANDSCAPE ARCHITECT Buro Lubbers
STABILITY DHV | Goudstikker de Vries
TECHNIQUES | ACOUSTICS Wolf Dikken Adviseurs
STRUCTURAL WORK Heijmans Woningbouw
AREA 10 500 m² COMPLETED November 2009
www.crepainbinst.be

AIBS 'FINCA' HOUSE
IBIZA | BALEARES | SPAIN
BRUNO ERPICUM & PARTNERS

TEXT Cécile Vandernoot
PHOTOGRAPHY Jean-Luc Laloux

The 'finca', the traditional house on Ibiza, consists of
a series of simple volumes organized around a patio.
Penetrating a property occurs in steps, as visitors, turning
corners and taking stairs, gradually wind their way into
the house. Once they have passed the front door, however,
the living area opens up unreservedly. While retaining the
essential features of this architectural grammar, Bruno
Erpicum also reinterprets certain of its aspects in his
clean-lined architecture. Bruno Erpicum built his first
island residence in 1988. "Since then, I have had almost
one commission per year. Projects are dictated by the plot
that will accommodate the house, while the landscape's
uncompromising beauty largely defines volumes and
openings". The Belgian architect has established a solid
reputation, and his modest approach has always been
well received by local administrations. His work has also
taken him further afield, however, and now, although the
firm is still based in Brussels, about half of its activities
occur outside Europe. "This geographic diversity is a great
source of satisfaction despite the many constraints we
face, such as integration and adaptation requirements, the
establishment and management of an economic branch in
each country, the red tape involved in joining the various
orders of architects, and the countless hours spent in
airports…" Located on the north of Ibiza, the Aibs house
sits atop a steep cliff, at an altitude of 159 metres. The first
hurdle the team encountered was persuading themselves
that excavation work was possible on this plot of land
that was both hostile and magnificent, and then proving
that it was also possible to integrate a project in harmony
with the natural surroundings. "The location of the plot
was amazing and constituted a real challenge for both the
building contractors and ourselves. In order to build there,
none of them could rely on their usual work methods:
neither cranes nor concrete trucks could be used, and all
materials had to be transported by van. On an island, more
than elsewhere, one has to make use of local resources
and call on local suppliers". Indeed, only they know where
to buy the best sand and how to make good concrete.

For over 20 years, Atelier d'Architecture Bruno Erpicum & Partners (AABE) has been building one residence per year on the island of Ibiza, all thanks to word of mouth.

AIBS HOUSE 'FINCA'
IBIZA | BALEARES | SPAIN
BRUNO ERPICUM & PARTNERS

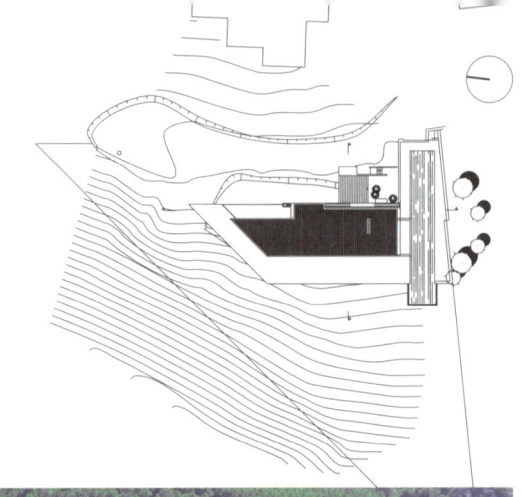

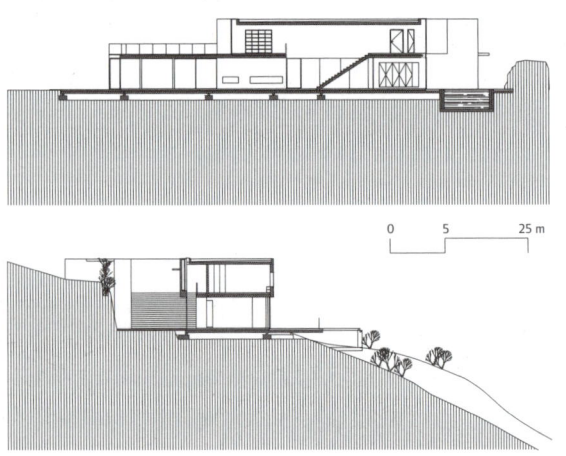

AIBS

PROGRAMME dwelling house PROCEDURE private

ARCHITECT Atelier d'Architecture Bruno Erpicum & Partners (AABE)

CLIENT Aibs STABILITY Beelen Engineering

STRUCTURAL WORK | FAÇADE | HEATING |

WORKMANSHIP OF INTERIOR Construcciones Bofibiza

CARPENTRY Carpenteria Gregorio ELECTRICITY Ituma

WORKMANSHIP OF EXTERIOR Technal | Carpenteria Mari Mari

AREA 400 m² BUDGET (excluding VAT and fees) 1 200 000 euro

COMPLETED July 2008

www.erpicum.org

ORDOS 100
ORDOS DESERT | INNER MONGOLIA | CHINA
JAN DE VYLDER ARCHITECTEN + WONNE ICKX
JDS ARCHITECTS + NU ARCHITECTUURATELIER + OFFICE KVGDS

TEXT Géraldine Michat
PHOTOGRAPHY Bert de Muynck

Coordinated by the artist, architect and Chinese dissident
Ai Weiwei and his firm Fake Design, the Ordos 100
project envisioned the building of 100 villas in a new city
in the Ordos desert of Inner Mongolia. A selection of 100
international architectural firms was made by Herzog &
de Meuron, among which were five Belgian teams. In
late January 2008, an initial meeting took place in the
city of Ordos, featuring NU Architectuuratelier, Jan De
Vylder Architecten, and Wonne Ickx of the Mexican firm
Productora (→ A+**211**). In April of that same year, Office
KGDVS and JDS Architects attended a second meeting
(→ A+**213**). Since then, it seems that the project manager
behind the undertaking is no longer on good terms
with the government authorities, and the – controver-
sial – project appears to have been halted: ordos.com
is now closed for "routine maintenance", while access
to ordosproject.com seems to be forbidden, the server
denying the specified URL.

Coordinated by the artist, architect and Chinese dissident Ai Weiwei and his firm Fake Design, the Ordos 100 project envisioned the building of 100 villas in a new city in the Ordos desert of Inner Mongolia, but the project appears to have been halted.

PASSIVE COUNCIL HOUSES
OIGNIES | FRANCE
R²D² ARCHITECTURE

TEXT Cécile Vandernoot
PHOTOGRAPHY R²D² Architecture

The firm's participation in the competition was quite unusual: delegates of the project manager (Pas-de-Calais Habitat) travelled to Brussels to assess the work of several firms with buildings setting new levels of excellence in terms of passive architecture. R²D² was soon invited to enter the competition, and that is how the firm was first confronted with the strict building regulations applied in France. "The site is a listed historical monument and a candidate for the Unesco World Heritage list. An open dialogue preceded the submission of the building permit application, which was, surprisingly, obtained without any difficulty. However", Vincent Szpirer recognizes, "I was not expecting to have to follow surface and budget require-ments so drastically. We called on an economist, the equivalent of a quantity surveyor, to help guide us".
The project is located on a former mining site, and the local economic revival is drawing new inhabitants, hence the competition. Its theme – 'living in a park' – refers essen-tially to the landscaping that was necessary to develop the area – a plot of land located between the slag heap and the Declercq garden-city – and its access points. The firm had to be creative without losing sight of the site's essential elements. "The position of the terraced houses was influenced by the decision to retain cones of vision and paths leading to the listed landscape. It was stipulated that the notion of private property was to be erased and

that this type of housing be achieved, although increased density would have been recommended for passive archi-tecture". That is why the small houses are semi-detached, in order to optimize surfaces and thereby save money. "The budget is well below what is done in Belgium, although it is a costly project for this public-housing authority". In terms of volume, the houses form a symbolic extension of the land. The north-facing sides are covered in dark grey zinc with regular openings. The south-facing sides feature large windows, and the living room gives out onto the park, and not onto a private garden. The mineralized pathways fade into the landscape, which literally absorbs those elements that are too domesticated. The vegetalization of the houses' sides also contributes to the integration of the houses in the landscape. "We drew on the exemplary local expertise in matters of rain-water management. As regards the market procurement, established in a competitive dialogue, there are also many things we could learn. The building contractors receive extremely detailed plans, but can consider building the project according to the method they believe is most effective, depending on the budget/ objective defined by the client. This puts them under the obligation to achieve the goals that have been set. The choice of the building contractor then follows the same procedure as for public architecture markets in Belgium".

"35 passive council houses to be built in Oignies, Pas-de-Calais": a public architecture competition won by R²D² Architecture, a firm that has made passive architecture its specialty.

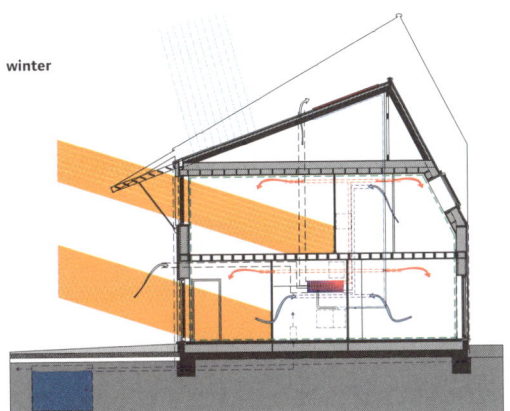

winter

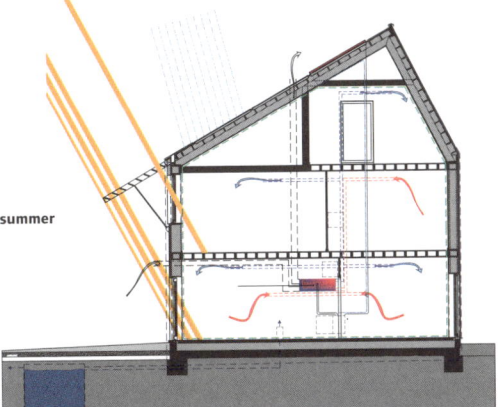

summer

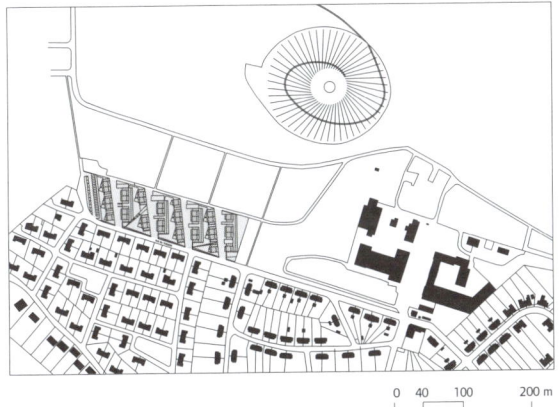

0   40   100   200 m

Passive council houses

PROGRAMME sustainable district for 35 passive council houses
PROCEDURE competition ARCHITECT | LANDSCAPE ARCHITECT R²D²
Architecture CLIENT Pas-de-Calais Habitat
EPB Energelio | Synapse Ingénierie
BUILDING CONTRACTOR Entreprise Sueur
MONITORING OFFICE Socotec ROADS SYSTEM AND
URBAN PUBLIC UTILITIES B&R Ingénierie Pas-de-Calais
AREA 5730 m² (gross) BUDGET (excluding VAT and fees) 6 500 000 euro
COMPLETED 2013
www.r2d2architecture.be

MAISON DU LAC
LAKE BOURGET | FRANCE
V+ BUREAU VERS PLUS DE BIEN-ÊTRE

TEXT Cécile Vandernoot
PHOTOGRAPHY 354 photographers

Having landed on their desk through a relative, this project led the architectural firm V+ to take on the challenge of the stereotypical French 'maison bourgeoise', built on a base and oriented according to the cardinal points. Although generously proportioned and coherently laid out, were one to ignore the incredible landscape surrounding it, it could be set in any wealthy suburb. "We sometimes like to sum up this project as follows: the original house was a hopelessly rigid bourgeoise, who needed to be liberated by our intervention".

The owner's initial request centred on the creation of a spacious kitchen destined to become the epicentre of activity, a living area that would communicate between both the indoors and outdoors. However, since the very thought of an extension generally leads to an examination of the house's potential but also of its aberrations, and since time was not an issue – the project matured over the course of three years – a mere extension developed into a full renovation.

"We met with the local decision-making authorities so that they could explain their work method to us and this, long before we had formulated anything in detail. They thus became very involved from the start and were surprisingly supportive". The house being set in a triply protected area, town planning regulations stipulate that any new volume must be in the Savoyard style and must fit in the continuation of the house's existing roofs (here at 45°). "Had we followed these regulations, the height under the roof in the kitchen would have been 10 metres, so it was easy to show that that was nonsensical". Proceeding by reductio ad absurdum thus made sense. "The architecture of the kitchen, the piano room, the terrace and the bedrooms nested below is the manifestation of a new formal grammar. It emerges from the house itself". Counterbalancing the extensions became necessary so that they would not seem protean, but logical. "It is as logic as a Swiss army knife when it is opened. Our formal research was based on a spatial analysis that took into account the views, the landscape's remarkable features,

the existing circulation, and the features of the house that were to be preserved".

The shell of the building was completed in six months, with the architects visiting the site every two weeks. But their presence was required for the two months needed for completion. "There is nothing luxurious in this house, neither exorbitant materials nor expensive bathroom installations; it is simply the quality of the volumes and the detailed finishings that generate the real added value of architecture".

'liberated house'

'hopelessly rigid house'

Maison du Lac is an astonishing summer residence on the shore of Lake Bourget. Its sculptural figure was authorized by town planning regulations as strict as they are subjective. The house is the first project built in France by the architectural firm V+.

MAISON DU LAC
LAKE BOURGET | FRANCE
V+ BUREAU VERS PLUS DE BIEN-ÊTRE

RESIDENTIAL

THERE IS NOTHING LUXURIOUS IN THIS
HOUSE. IT IS SIMPLY THE QUALITY OF
THE VOLUMES AND THE DETAILED
FINISHINGS THAT GENERATE THE REAL
ADDED VALUE OF ARCHITECTURE.

MAISON DU LAC
LAKE BOURGET | FRANCE
V+ BUREAU VERS PLUS DE BIEN-ÊTRE

basement

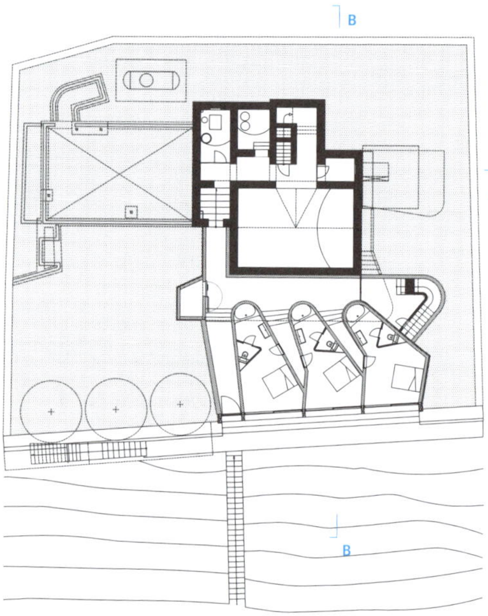

B

A ⌐ ⌐ A

B

ground floor

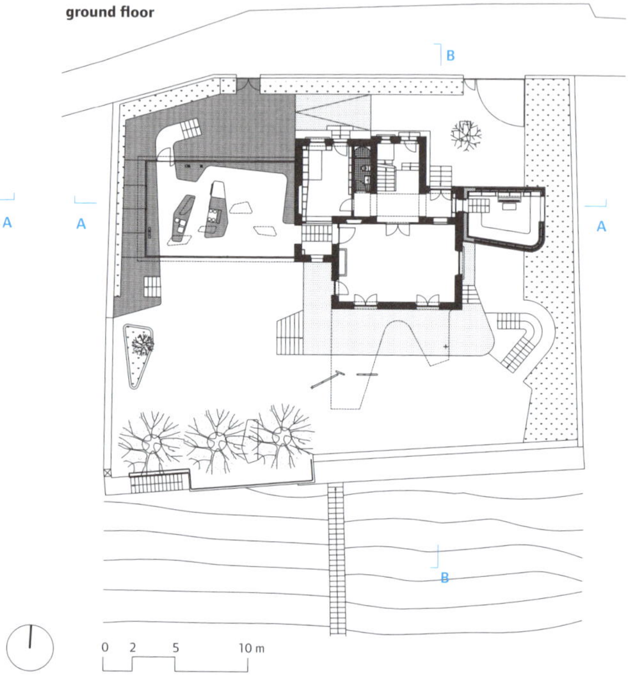

B

A ⌐ ⌐ A

B

0 2   5   10 m

OUR FORMAL RESEARCH WAS BASED ON A
SPATIAL ANALYSIS THAT TOOK INTO ACCOUNT
THE VIEWS, THE LANDSCAPE'S REMARKABLE
FEATURES, THE EXISTING CIRCULATION, AND
THE FEATURES OF THE HOUSE THAT WERE TO
BE PRESERVED.

section A

section B

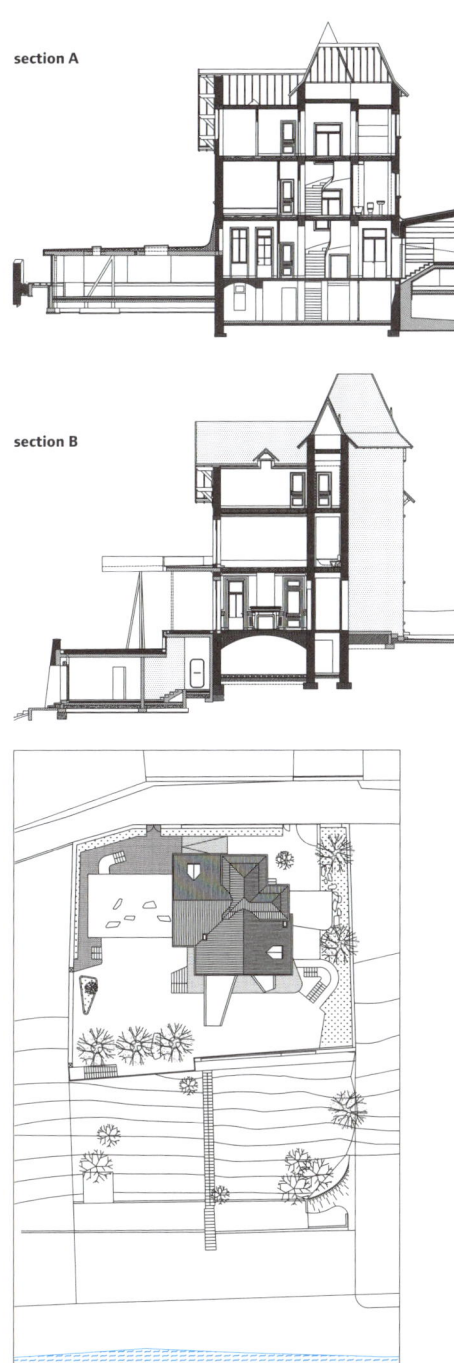

Maison du Lac

PROGRAMME extension and renovation of a
single family house PROCEDURE private
ARCHITECT V+ bureau vers plus de bien-être | Antoine Rocca
CLIENT private STABILITY Bollinger + Grohmann | Secoba
TECHNIQUES | ACOUSTICS Daidalos Peutz STRUCTURAL WORK Léon Grosse
CARPENTRY John Cochet Charpente | Les Bois Riant | Menuiserie Gaillard
FAÇADE Barbier ELECTRICITY ND&NH HEATING ESB
WORKMANSHIP OF INTERIOR Atelier C IRON FORGE Yves Pellegrin
AREA before 330 m² net | afterwards 550 m² net | site 5000 m²
COMPLETED July 2011
www.vplus.org

© Elina Brotherus

BO ZAR EX PO

14.06 > 16.09.2012

Sense of Place
European Landscape Photography

PALEIS VOOR
SCHONE KUNSTEN,
BRUSSEL

PALAIS
DES BEAUX-ARTS,
BRUXELLES

CENTRE
FOR FINE ARTS,
BRUSSELS

WWW.BOZAR.BE | + 32 (0)2 507 82 00

 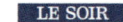 

Bauwelt

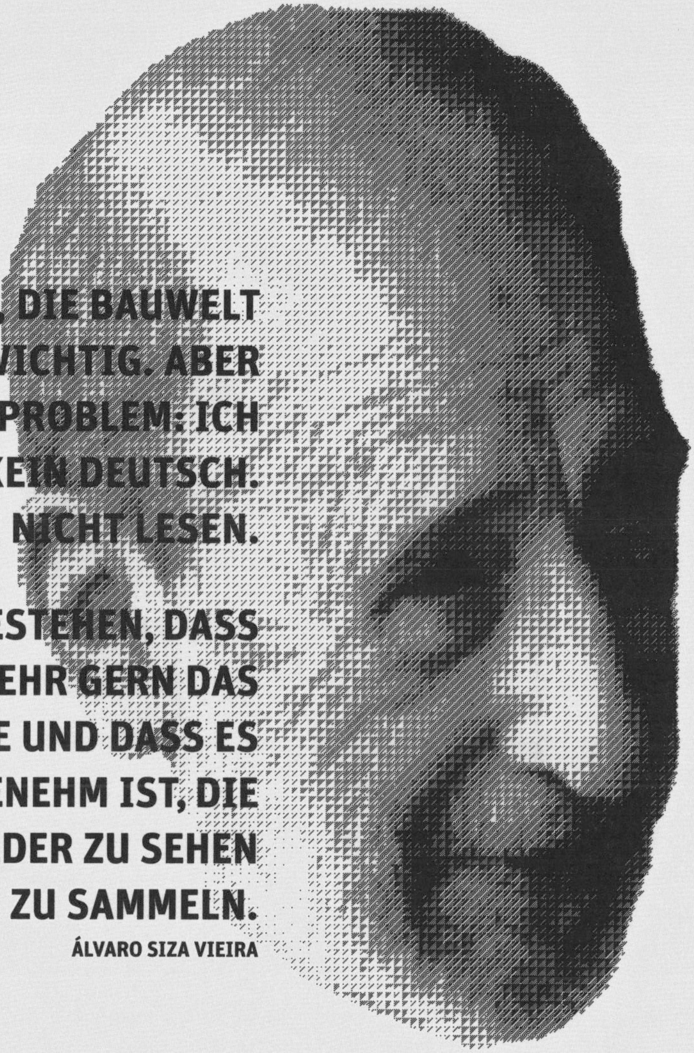

KEIN ZWEIFEL, DIE BAUWELT
IST WICHTIG. ABER
ICH HABE EIN PROBLEM: ICH
VERSTEHE KEIN DEUTSCH.
ICH KANN SIE NICHT LESEN.

ICH MUSS GESTEHEN, DASS
ICH SEHR GERN DAS
PAPIER ANFASSE UND DASS ES
SEHR ANGENEHM IST, DIE
GEDRUCKTEN BILDER ZU SEHEN
UND DIE HEFTE ZU SAMMELN.
ÁLVARO SIZA VIEIRA

ORIGINAL IMAGE © SINAE

HOUSING PROJECT
BORDEAUX | FRANCE

51N4E | GRAU

TEXT Benjamin Pors
PHOTOGRAPHY 51N4E | GRAU

From the moment the firm was founded, the architects of 51N4E have taken on projects abroad. They are currently at work in Switzerland, Albania, Germany and France. "The decision to undertake these projects is due to the interest these commissions generate", explains Freek Persyn, one of the firm's three associates. The team is also eager to collaborate with foreign firms. "Collaborating with firms adds a certain richness to the project. The foreign office always has a more intuitive knowledge while that of the local office is more operational". To respond to the call for projects issued by the Urban Community of Bordeaux (CUB), 51N4E thus formed an association with the French town-planning firm GRAU. This call for projects aimed to outline imaginative strategies for the construction of the city with an eye on sustainable development. The objective of this process is to create an intervention framework that will make it possible to limit urban sprawling and promote the construction of qualitative and lasting housing units. The reflection process lasted six months and was followed by a technical committee of experts and a political committee consisting of the mayors of the districts that make up the agglomeration. This political presence from the start of the process made it possible to establish a link between the theoretical reflection and the tangible execution of projects.

The team's approach revolves around an action plan in three movements: a contextual analysis, the definition of the intervention methods, and the identification of strategic sections of the territory for the implementation of the plan. The first movement centres on the identification of the territorial characteristics of Bordeaux. The architects then explored 'territorial strategies', possible visions for the transformation of this contextual reality following four hypotheses: the vision of the city as a residential area within a mobility network; territorial predominance, or the hypothesis that peripheral zones are as important as the centre; the idea of scales of diversity, or the importance of implementing specific solutions to preserve the intrinsic characteristics of certain areas; lastly, the notion of horizontal and emergent density, and the importance of maintaining a contrast in the interpretation of the territory.

The concrete implementation of the plan involves the identification of four strategic types of territorial zones: clusters, or the concentration or polarization of potentially developable sites; amenities, or plots linked to natural areas; poles, or land reserves close to monofunctional zones such as a campus or ecoparc; micro-operations, or more widely scattered but numerous zones. The four forms of territories that were identified enable a simultaneous implementation of the plan according to different proportions and rhythms.

This approach gives the expansion plan an analytical framework that is transposable to a multitude of geographic inscriptions. It defines local implementation possibilities and fits in a reflection on the future of the global urban community.

50 000 housing units around collective transport axes

PROGRAMME urban strategy for the distribution and realization of 50 000 new homes
PROCEDURE competition by invitation ARCHITECT 51N4E | GRAU
CLIENT Communauté Urbaine de Bordeaux (CUB)
LANDSCAPE ARCHITECT Thierry Laverne
CONSULTANT ECONOMY IDEA Consult CONSULTANT SUSTAINABILITY 3E
CONSULTANT STRATEGY | CONSULTANT URBANISM Dominique Boudet
COMPLETED April 2012
www.lacub.fr

51N4E is one of the five teams chosen in the context of the call for projects for '50 000 new housing units clustered around public transport axes' in Bordeaux. An interview with architect Freek Persyn.

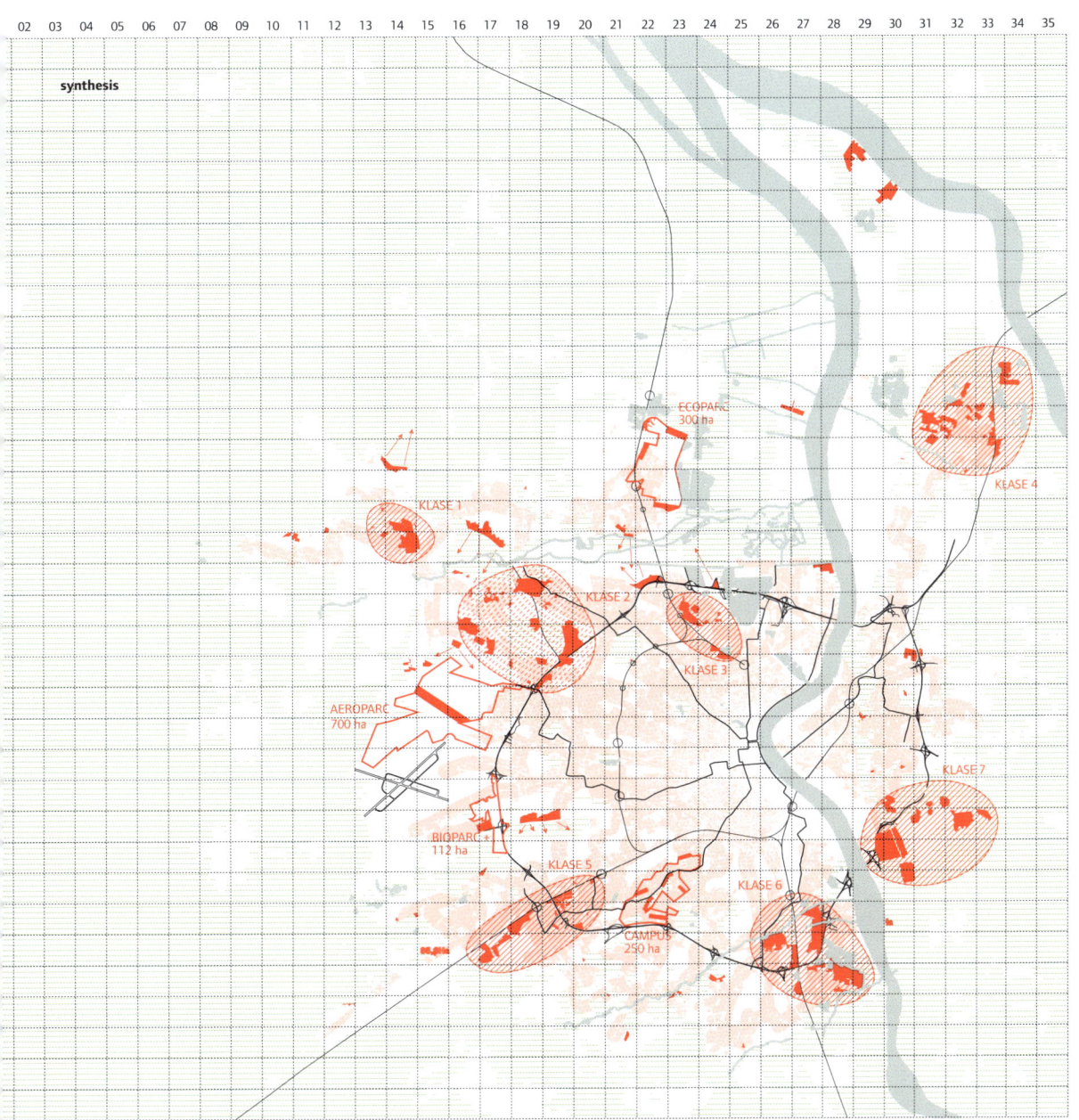

02 03 04 05 06 07 08 09 10 11 12 13 14 15 16 17 18 19 20 21 22 23 24 25 26 27 28 29 30 31 32 33 34 35

synthesis

ECOPARC
300 ha

KLASE 4

KLASE 1

KLASE 2

KLASE 3

AEROPARC
700 ha

KLASE 7

BIOPARC
112 ha

KLASE 5

KLASE 6

CAMPUS
250 ha

HOUSING PROJECT
BORDEAUX | FRANCE
51N4E | GRAU

hypothesis

scales of diversity

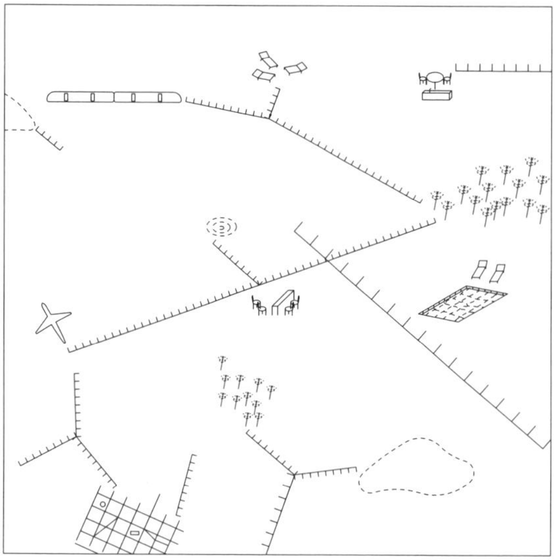

horizontal and emergent densities

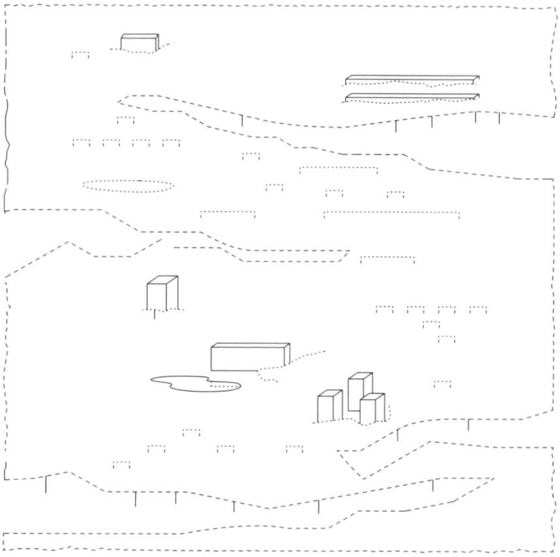

housing + transport = city

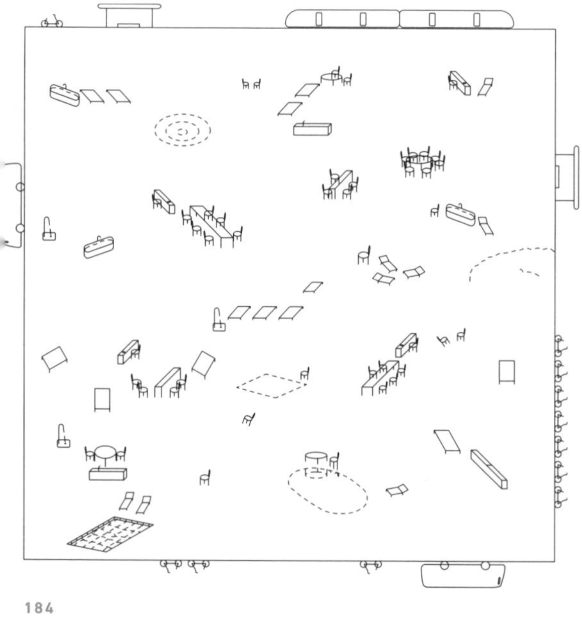

territorial predominance

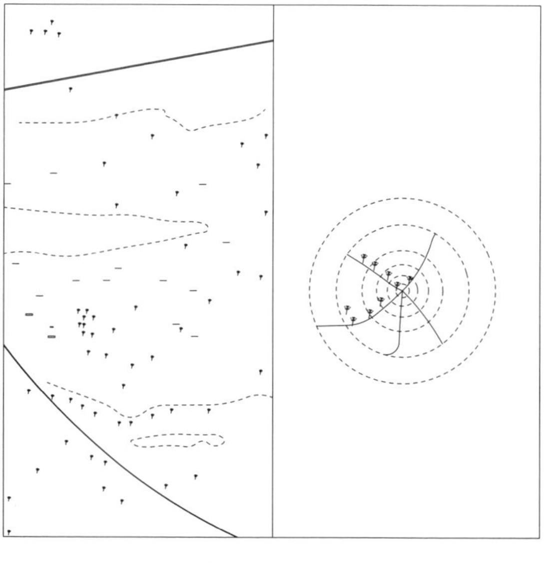

THIS CALL FOR PROJECTS AIMED TO
OUTLINE IMAGINATIVE STRATEGIES FOR THE
CONSTRUCTION OF THE CITY WITH AN EYE ON
SUSTAINABLE DEVELOPMENT.

territorial strategy

clusters

amenities

poles

micro-operations

HOUSING PROJECT
BORDEAUX | FRANCE
51N4E | GRAU

architectural strategy (horizontal density)

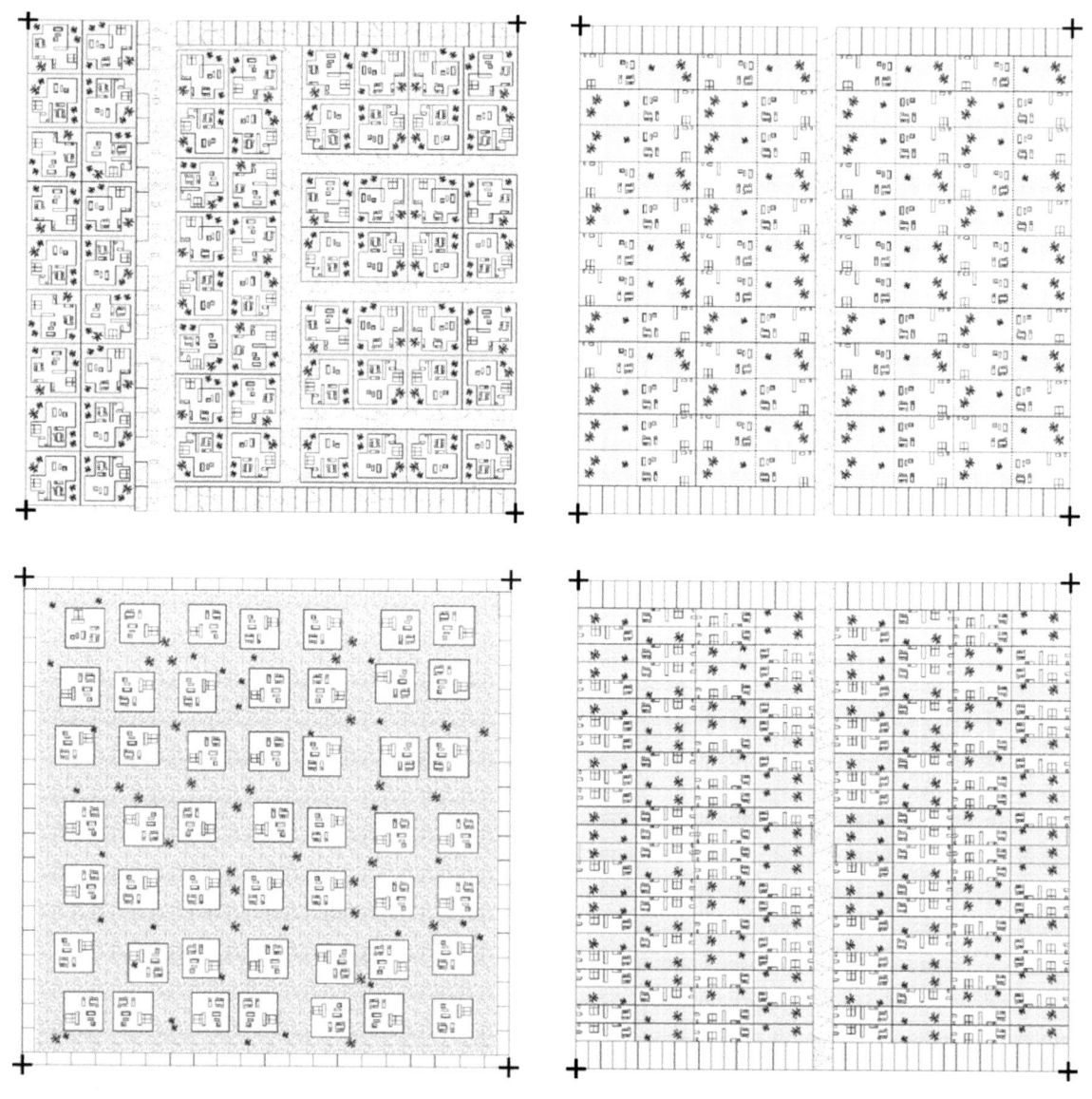

URBAN PLANNING

FROM THE MOMENT THE FIRM WAS FOUNDED,
THE ARCHITECTS OF 51N4E HAVE TAKEN ON
PROJECTS ABROAD. THEY ARE CURRENTLY AT
WORK IN SWITZERLAND, ALBANIA, GERMANY
AND FRANCE.

architectural strategy (emergent density)

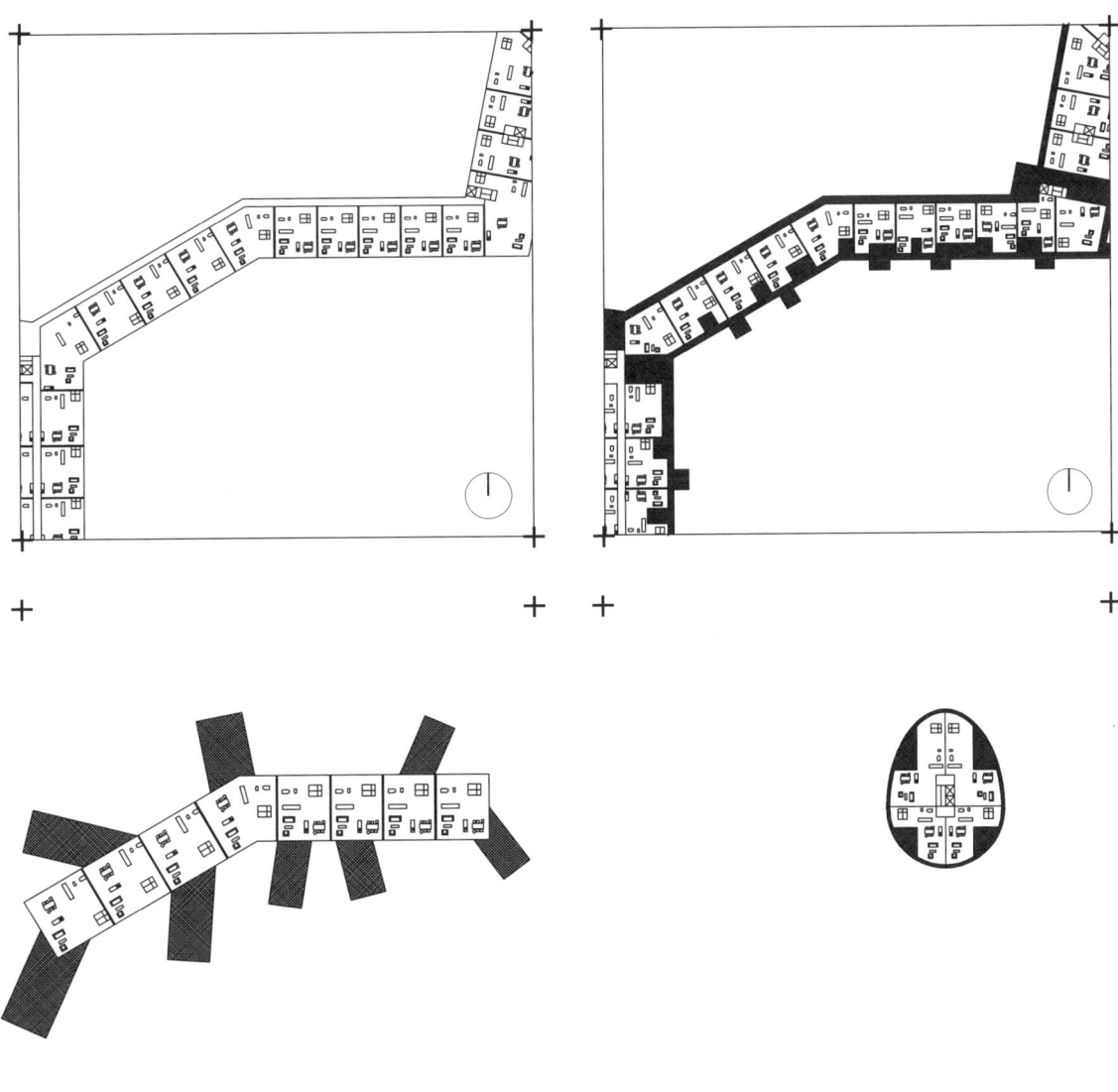

MANZO IBI VILLAGE
IBI-BATEKE | D.R. CONGO
BOGDAN & VAN BROECK ARCHITECTS

TEXT Dieter Van Den Storm
PHOTOGRAPHY Bogdan & Van Broeck Architects

Located some 200 km outside Kinshasa, the domain on the Bateke highlands stretches over 22 000 hectares, an area slightly larger than the Brussels-Capital Region. A few years ago the sound of gunfire still resonated around here, but the region is now fully devoted to reconstruction. The ecological project that attracted Bogdan & Van Broeck Architects involves the development of a newly inaugurated carbon sink. The project has notably received the support of international institutions such as the World Bank, Umicore, Suez-Tractebel, and of various NGOs. "This project has generated a number of parallel effects", explains Leo Van Broeck. "There is a section devoted to subsistence economy such as the small-scale cassava industry which should ensure employment. The biodiversity is being reinforced by the protection and extension of the rainforest, and socio-cultural projects include the construction of villages, schools and medical dispensaries. In the long run, ecological forestry will also be developed". Next to town-planning advice on the development of the site, the project manager also had a more concrete issue. "Besides the people who live and work there, the domain must also offer accommodation to the various guests expected there yearly", continues Leo Van Broeck. "That can be anything from VIPs and investors to World Bank employees or technicians measuring levels of CO_2. There is little to do in the region around Kinshasa. People wishing to do a bit of ecotourism must also be able to have that opportunity. So there is need for accommodation, even though it doesn't have to be a five-star hotel". The original idea, which was to convert an existing tobacco-drying barn into a two-floor guest lodge, seemed to be too expensive. In the end the choice went to a 100-metre long structure with a single floor, where the rooms are located in a single elongated block. This has made it possible to build in phases, depending on the state of the financial resources. The cost and availability of materials was not only a source of concern, but also a source of inspiration. "The building sector relies on what is to be had at the village market", says Van Broeck.

"This means that you have to be creative with whatever materials are available, such as sheets of corrugated iron, wood beams, or stabilized-earth bricks that serve to build dividing walls".
That the DNA of each location and each commission varies radically is something all architects know. "With this project it really was quite specific", concludes Van Broeck. "It is a very context-related project, and nothing from this project will be added to our portfolio to serve our next projects. We are also doing this largely free of charge. There is no budget and they are currently not generating any revenue. We hope to get part of our fee retroactively. So it is a bit of development aid, and for us a long-term investment. I hope we get more work abroad out of it".

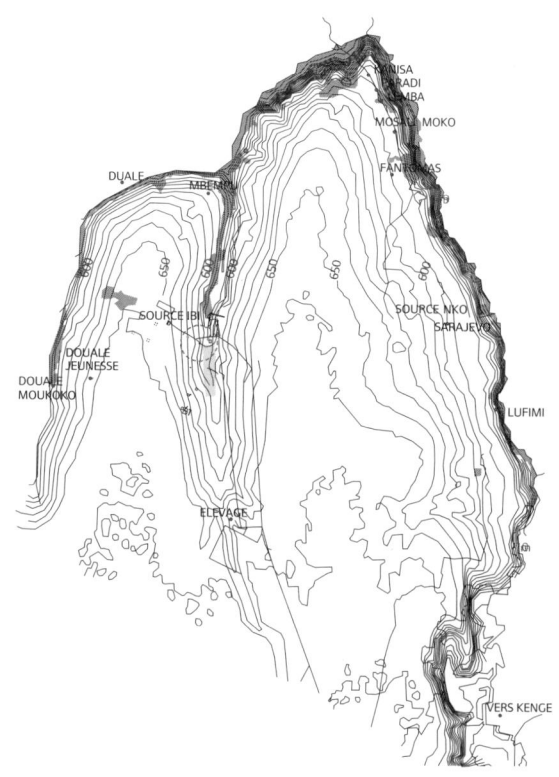

The building of a guest lodge in the Democratic Republic of Congo is the first African venture of Bogdan & Van Broeck Architects. This poetic but contextual project at times bears a close resemblance to development aid, as the Brussels-based architects themselves recognize.

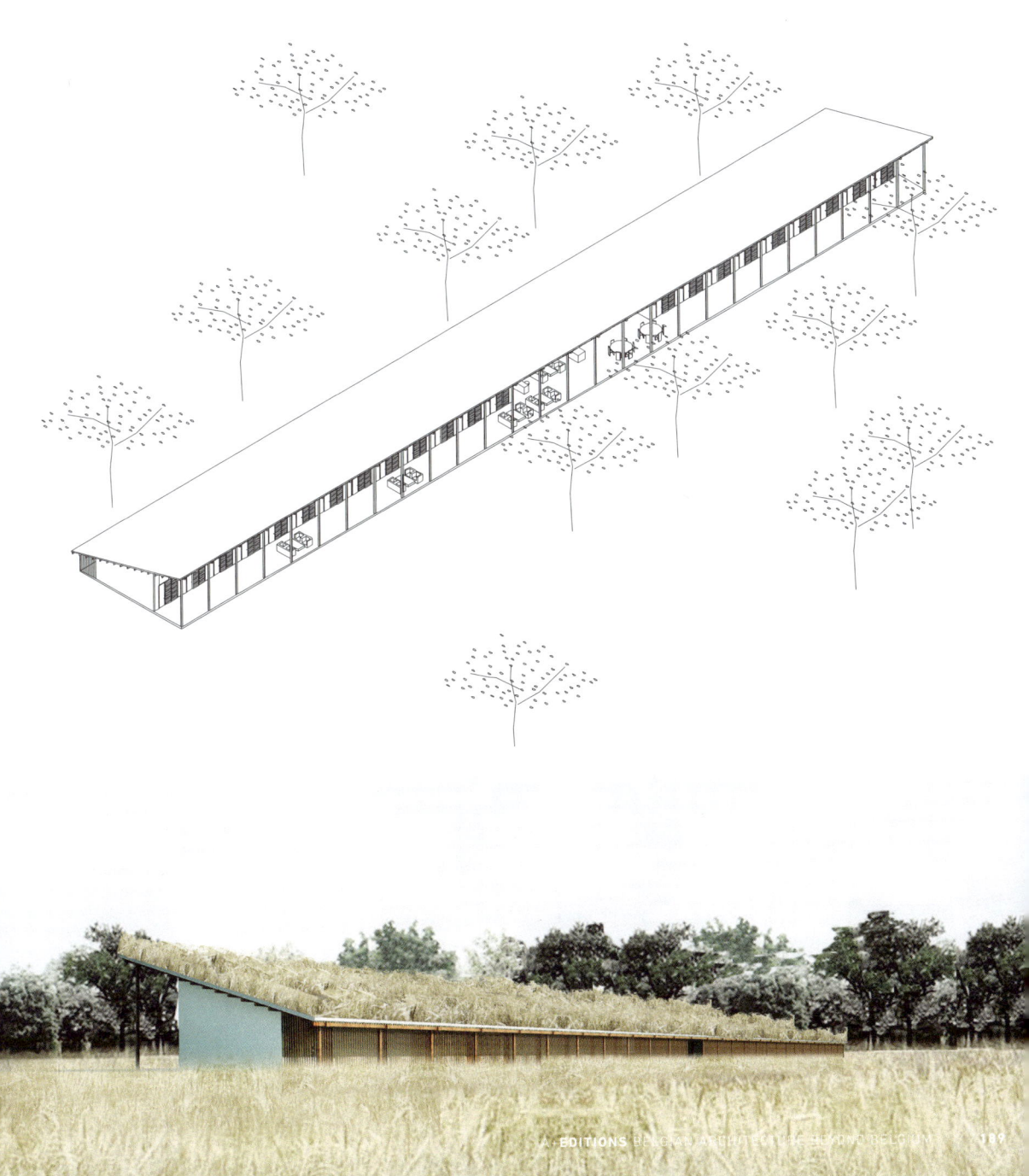

MANZO IBI VILLAGE
IBI-BATEKE | D.R. CONGO
BOGDAN & VAN BROECK ARCHITECTS

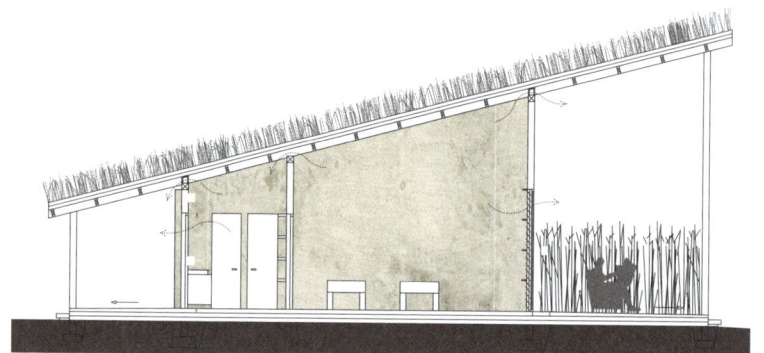

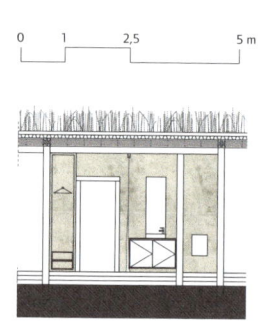

0 1   2,5   5 m

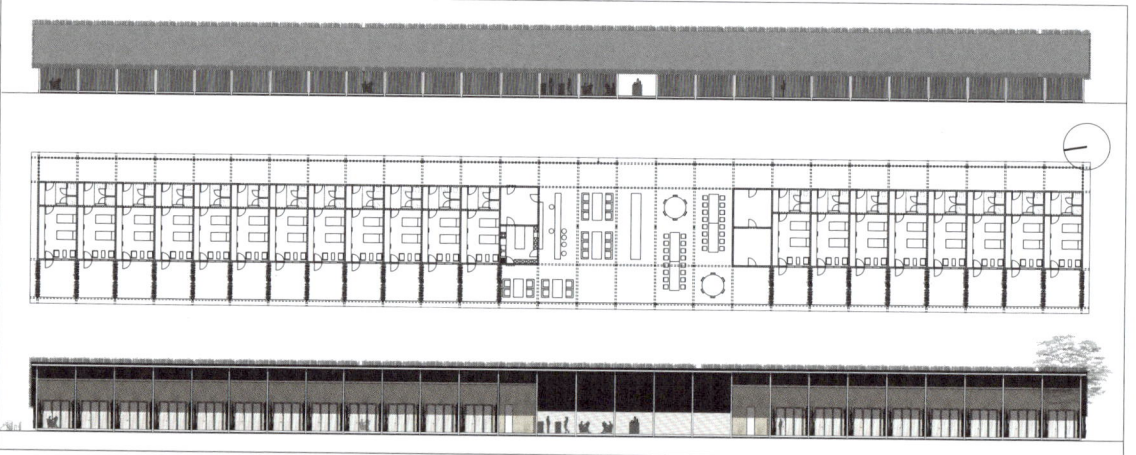

Manzo Ibi Village

PROGRAMME accommodation for international guests PROCEDURE private
ARCHITECT Bogdan & Van Broeck Architects
CLIENT Ibi Village, Mbankana, Kinshasa, DR Congo STABILITY | TECHNIQUES Bogdan & Van Broeck Architects STRUCTURAL WORK | CARPENTRY | FAÇADE| ELECTRICITY| HEATING | WORKMANSHIP OF INTERIOR local workers
AREA 589 m² (gross)
BUDGET (excluding VAT and fees) 300 000 euro
COMPLETED 2013
www.ibi-village.cd | www.bvbarchitects.com

MOULINET SITE MASTER PLAN
AULT | FRANCE
SUMRESEARCH

TEXT Gilles Béchet
PHOTOGRAPHY SumResearch

When a project involves transforming and moving a settlement that has developed over many years, the operation is a complex one since one has to take into account not only the architecture but also the social fabric and its integration in the landscape. In Ault, a city on the coast of Picardy in which the seaside houses are being threatened by the erosion of the chalk cliffs, the municipal authorities have decided to urbanize a vast protected site in the city centre, the Moulinet site, notably in order to rehouse the inhabitants. The elaboration of the master plan for the development of the new site was the subject of a public tender offer, won by SumResearch. This invitation owes nothing to chance, but to the presence of the firm in northern France for the past two decades. It all started in Saint-Valéry-sur-Somme with a competition for the urban renovation of the city centre in which SumResearch took part together with JNC International. One of their first realizations was the construction of a landing stage which, by means of a promenade, brings the city centre closer to the Baie de Somme. "That project was a turning point", says Paul Lievevrouw, an architect and the firm's director. "It enabled us to gain the inhabitants' confidence and be recognized in our town-planning advisory mission". The skills developed by SumResearch's multidisciplinary team, comprising architects, sociologists and town planners, were new in France. They were the fruit of experience acquired in Bruges where, as early as 1972, SumResearch elaborated and followed up a structural plan to regenerate the historic city and adapt the public space to the new functions of a modern city. "In Ault, our mission consisted in creating a town-planning framework that determines a general direction and takes into account criteria for a lasting development and the value of the heritage, and makes it possible to determine the feasibility of architectural projects on the site". To refine its project, the SumResearch team did not limit itself to architectural, town-planning and landscaping features, but conducted an in-depth analysis of the region's social fabric. For this, SumResearch was able to draw on the experience

notably acquired through neighbourhood redevelopment contracts in Brussels. While the French welcomed the quality of the outside vision offered by the Belgians, the latter discovered new work methods and learned how to conduct discussions with local committees. "In France, one knows from the start which way the decision will go and there is no turning back, while here in Belgium one must often seek out the truth from among divergent opinions". Having drafted the master plan for the Moulinet site, SumResearch also ensures the follow-up of the project. The current morose economic context has delayed the beginning of the work. "We are there to ensure the overall coherence so that even if smaller projects are launched, we will make sure they fit in the master plan and present the same level of quality". Boris Huyghebaert and Livia de Béthune thus ensure the follow-up of the various missions conducted by SumResearch in the north of France.

It took some in-depth research in Ault, Picardy, for the architectural firm SumResearch to fit a new housing settlement into a protected heritage site. For this complex town-planning job, an integrated team of architects, sociologists and town planners ensured that both quality of life and the landscape were preserved.

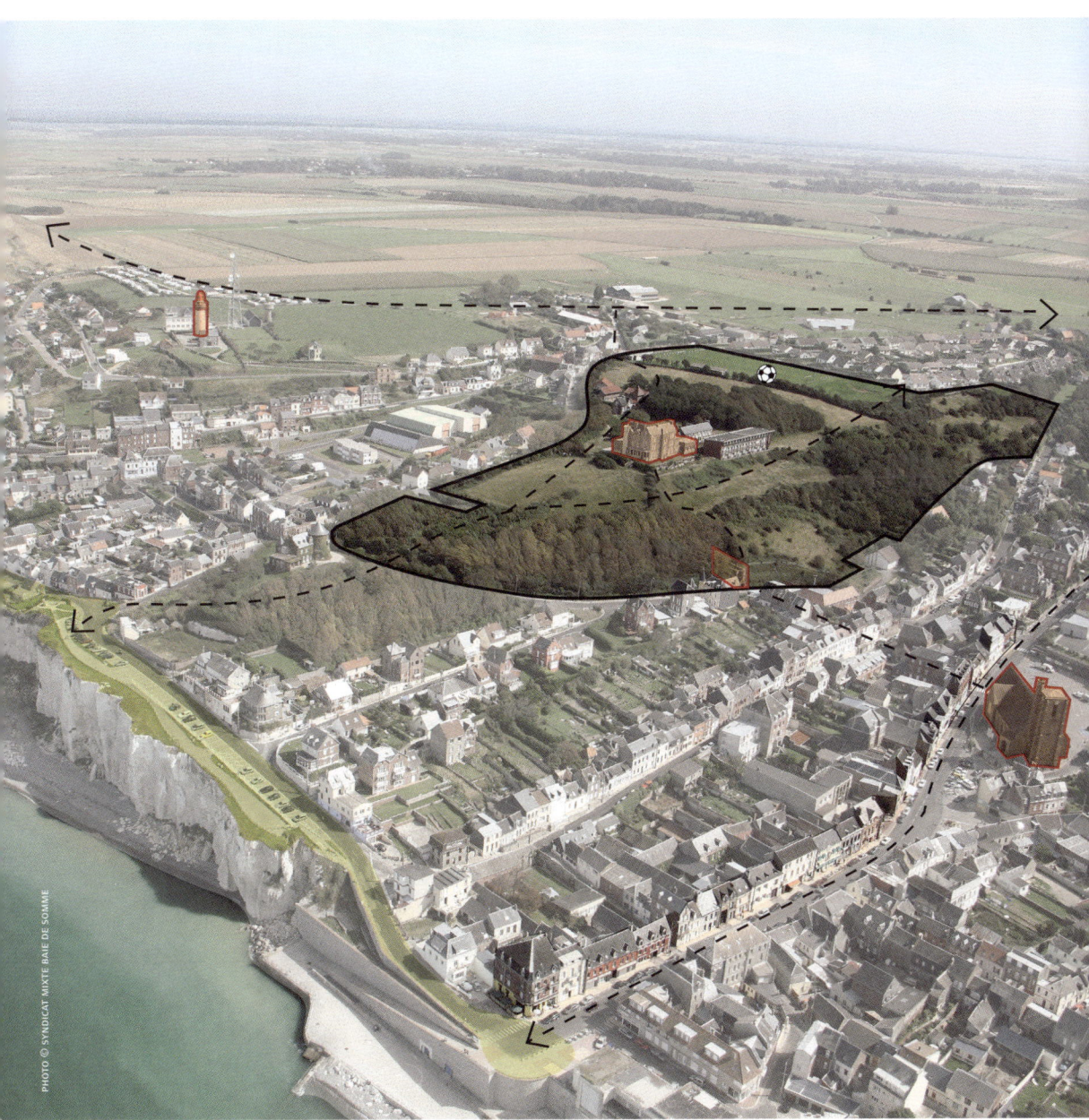

PHOTO © SYNDICAT MIXTE BAIE DE SOMME

MOULINET SITE MASTER PLAN
AULT | FRANCE
SUMRESEARCH

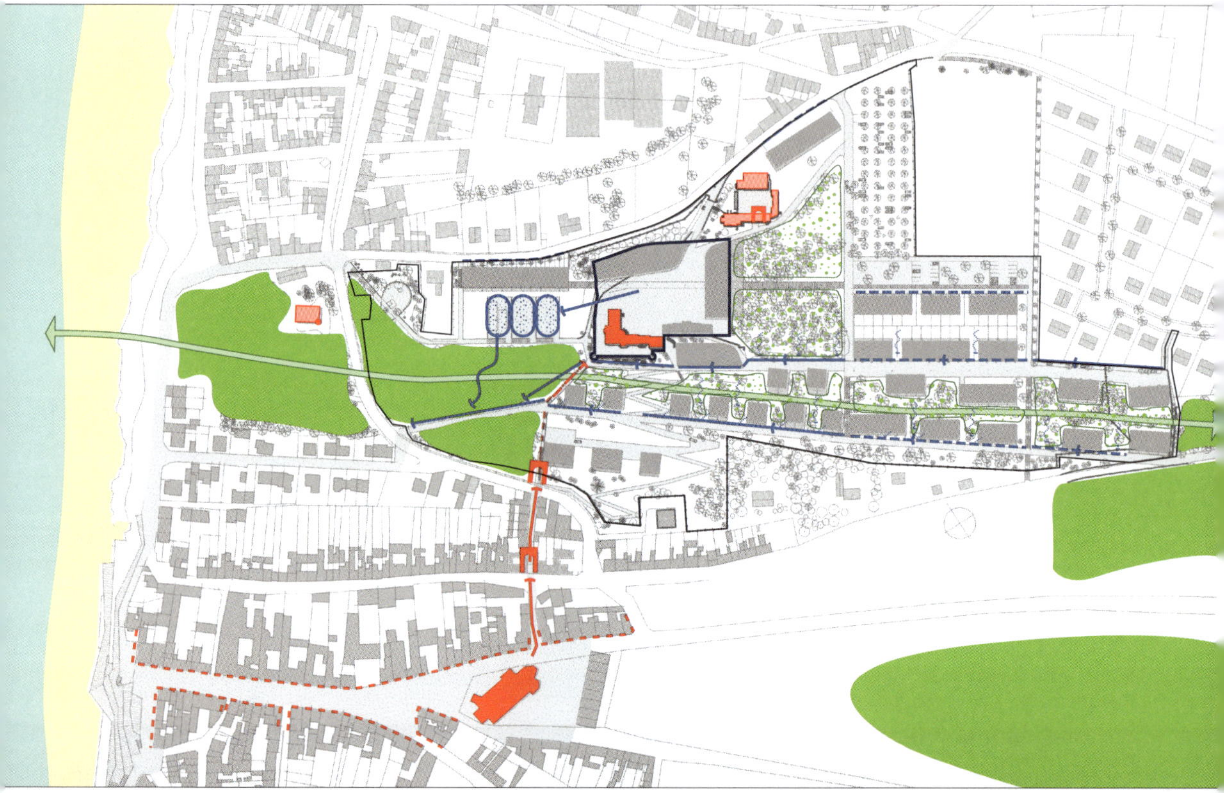

**sustainable
approach**

PHOTO © SYNDICAT MIXTE BAIE DE SOMME

IN AULT, A SEASIDE TOWN THREATENED
BY THE EROSION OF THE CHALK CLIFFS,
THE MUNICIPAL AUTHORITIES DECIDED TO
URBANIZE A VAST PROTECTED SITE IN THE CITY
CENTRE, THE MOULINET SITE.

Ault before 1950

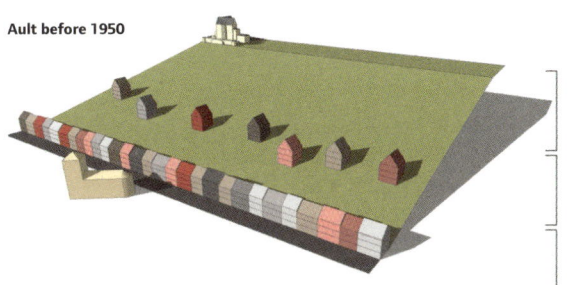

site

second line
3 floors

centre
2-4 floors

**Ault after 2010
scenario A**

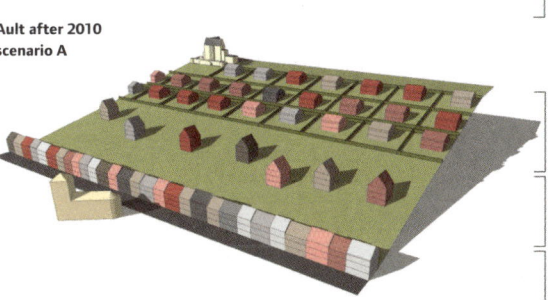

detached house
1-2 floors

second line
3 floors

centre
2-4 floors

**Ault after 2010
scenario B**

façade
2-4 floors

second line
3 floors

centre
2-4 floors

**Ault after 2010
scenario C**

pavilion
2-3 floors

second line
3 floors

centre
2-4 floors

Moulinet Site master plan

PROGRAMME sustainable master plan and
monitoring implementation (dwellings,
reception hall, hotel and public infrastructure)
PROCEDURE competition in the context
of an urban development zone
ARCHITECT SumResearch CLIENT Syndicat
Mixte Baie de Somme – Grand Littoral Picard
ARCHITECT | URBANIST SumResearch in
collaboration with VERDI Ingénierie + Sorepa
BUDGET (excluding VAT and fees)
approximately 55 000 000 euro
SURFACE 7 ha COMPLETED 2018
www.sum.be

MACDONALD WAREHOUSE CONVERSION
PARIS | FRANCE
XDGA | FAA

TEXT Dieter Van Den Storm
PHOTOGRAPHY XDGA

Located next to the Parc de la Villette on the boulevard Macdonald in the north-east of Paris, a vast, abandoned warehouse is currently being converted. The existing building measures 600 metres in length and was used as a storage space by the museums located on the Seine and by the police for impounded cars. New metro lines and an RER station should breathe new life into this remote quarter of Paris. "If Paris had been chosen to organize the 2012 Olympic Games, this building would have been the international press centre. Since London will have that privilege, this area has been given a new purpose, with offices, housing, shops and schools", explains Floris Alkemade of FAA. Alkemade, who was still working with OMA when the competition for this project was won, took this project with him when he left, and is now developing it with XDGA. Together they refined the master plan and are monitoring the overall coordination.

In 1968 already, the architect of the original building had anticipated the possibility that more floors could be added to the ground floor. The foundations and supporting structure are able to support several levels. That is why XDGA and FAA decided to preserve the building in its entirety. Their plan provides for six to seven new floors. Shops will occupy the ground floor, and a line will be drawn through the building for the new tram, around which a square with restaurants will be created.

"Despite the amazing length of the building, it is still on a human scale. There was no need to reduce it in size. You have to see it as an addition to the city with a lot of new opportunities", Alkemade continues. "We really have interpreted and presented it as an area of the city on which various architects are working. On top of the overall coordination, we are also in charge of the shops and two of the residential towers. Besides us, other architects are also involved, such as Christian de Portzamparc, Gigon Guyer Architects and Mia Hägg's Habiter Autrement". This is not the first time that XDGA is building in France. Most of the team is based in Brussels, but a team of four is overseeing the project in Paris. Now that construction is under way, meetings are held daily. An affinity with French culture and the ensuing command of French ensure there is no language barrier. And that plays fully to the advantage of the Brussels team.

"It was always obvious in a sense that we would work on projects abroad. I used to be with OMA and half of the projects there already took place abroad", concludes Xaveer De Geyter. "For me it is not a matter of leaving my own stamp. That will take care of itself. It is precisely collaborations that we seek. I now work with some 40 people. It is difficult to keep an office of that size busy with the Belgian market alone. Since the market has been slowing down in the Netherlands for a couple of years already, we now work quite a lot in France. One of the reasons for this is that competitions among our southern neighbours are well paid. That might be a base motivation, but it is realistic. Moreover, the French government plays an important role in keeping projects running".

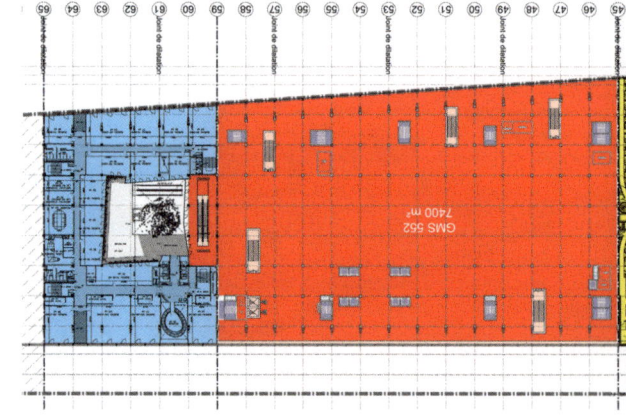

A brand new city quarter is emerging above an existing warehouse. The sophisticated master plan by XDGA and FAA provides for residential towers, offices and shops distributed over different levels. Thanks to the efforts of the authorities, such ambitious projects are still possible in France.

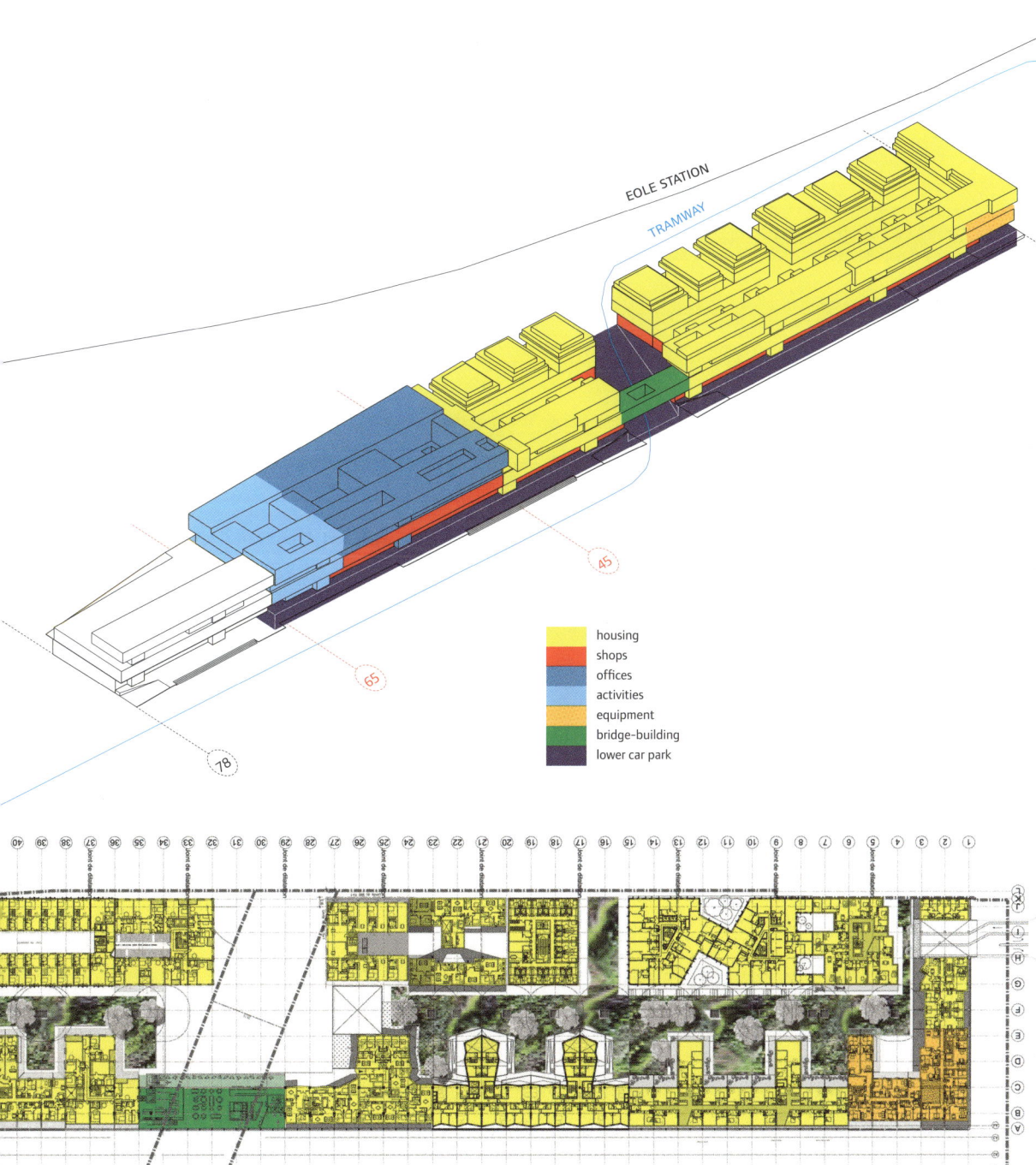

EOLE STATION

TRAMWAY

45

65

78

■	housing
■	shops
■	offices
■	activities
■	equipment
■	bridge-building
■	lower car park

MACDONALD WAREHOUSE CONVERSION
PARIS | FRANCE
XDGA | FAA

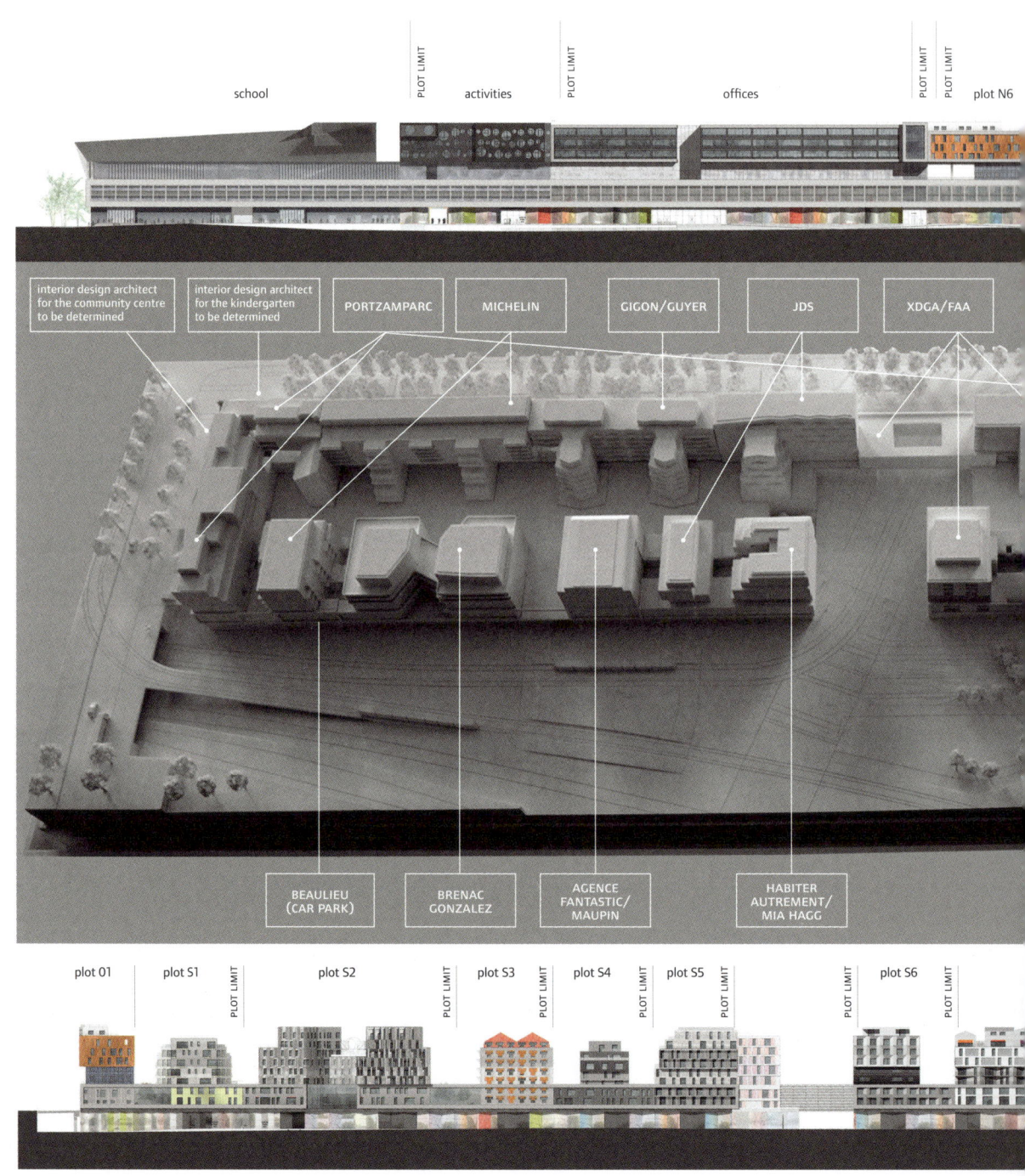

school · PLOT LIMIT · activities · PLOT LIMIT · offices · PLOT LIMIT · PLOT LIMIT · plot N6

interior design architect for the community centre to be determined · interior design architect for the kindergarten to be determined · PORTZAMPARC · MICHELIN · GIGON/GUYER · JDS · XDGA/FAA

BEAULIEU (CAR PARK) · BRENAC GONZALEZ · AGENCE FANTASTIC/ MAUPIN · HABITER AUTREMENT/ MIA HAGG

plot 01 · plot S1 · PLOT LIMIT · plot S2 · PLOT LIMIT · plot S3 · PLOT LIMIT · plot S4 · PLOT LIMIT · plot S5 · PLOT LIMIT · PLOT LIMIT · plot S6 · PLOT LIMIT

THE EXISTING BUILDING MEASURES 600
METRES IN LENGTH AND WAS USED AS A
STORAGE SPACE BY THE MUSEUMS LOCATED
ON THE SEINE AND BY THE POLICE FOR
IMPOUNDED CARS.

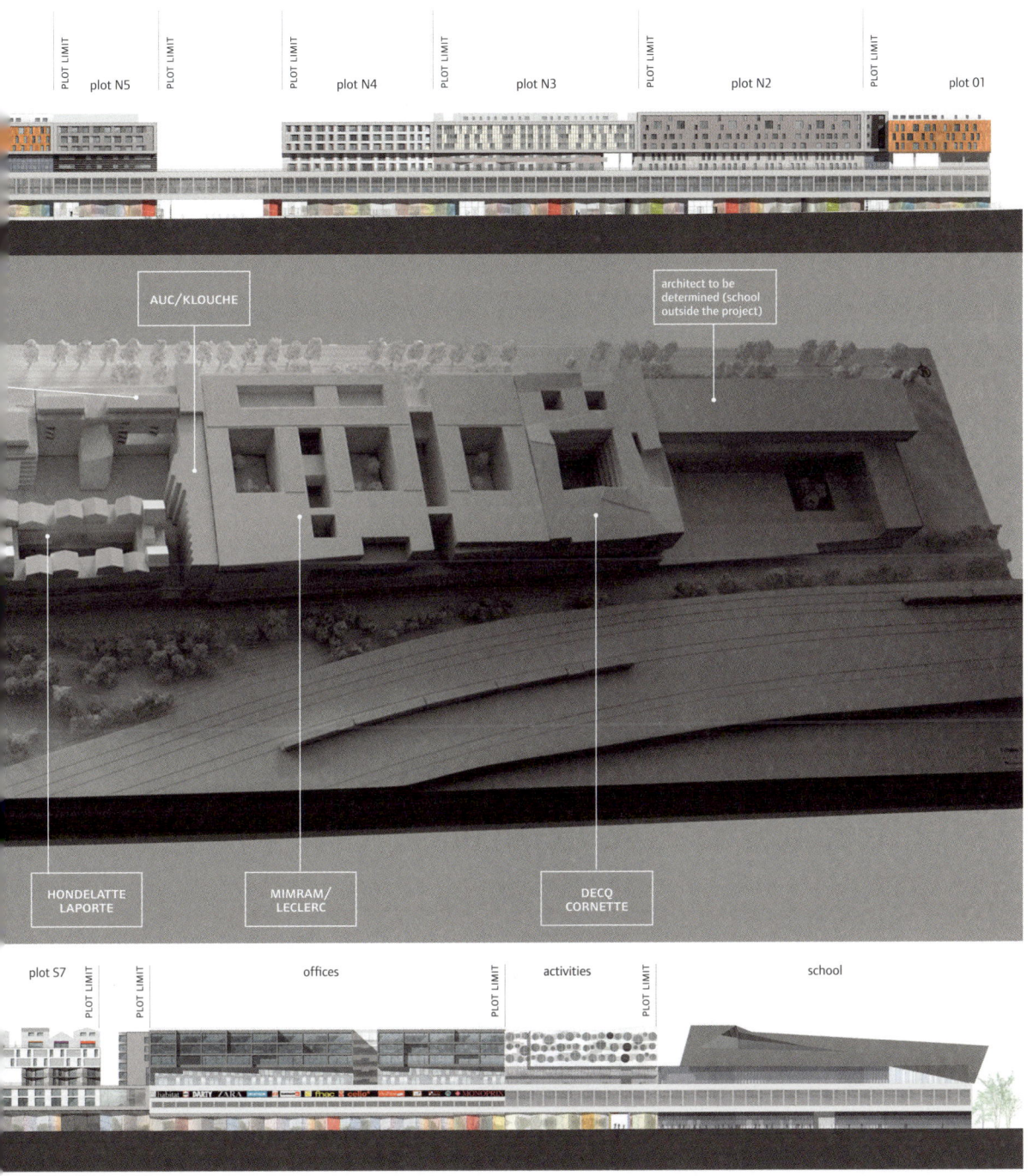

PLOT LIMIT   plot N5   PLOT LIMIT   PLOT LIMIT   plot N4   PLOT LIMIT   plot N3   PLOT LIMIT   plot N2   PLOT LIMIT   plot 01

AUC/KLOUCHE

architect to be
determined (school
outside the project)

HONDELATTE
LAPORTE

MIMRAM/
LECLERC

DECQ
CORNETTE

plot S7   PLOT LIMIT   PLOT LIMIT   offices   PLOT LIMIT   activities   PLOT LIMIT   school

© MARCEL FOREST ARCHITECT

Macdonald warehouse conversion

PROGRAMME rehabilitation of the old Macdonald warehouse into housing, offices, commercial spaces, facilities and car parks

PROCEDURE competition for a master plan, attribution of different programmes to selected architects (awarded to OMA, later taken over by FAA)

ARCHITECT XDGA | FAA CLIENT Paris Nord-Est

LANDSCAPE ARCHITECT Michel Desvignes

STABILITY | TECHNIQUES BET Setec

EPB Franck Boutté Consultants ACOUSTICS AVLS

STRUCTURE (SHELL) SICRA (Groupe Vinci) HEATING CPCU

SURFACE 165 000 m² net surface area

COMPLETED September 2014

www.xdga.be

PREPARATION AND MODERATION OF THE DISCUSSION
Audrey Contesse and Pieter T'Jonck

Aurore Boraczek

Audrey Contesse

Oswald Dellicour

Carl Destoop

Aurore Boraczek holds a degree in Romance languages and literature. In 2004, following a research contract with the University of Liège, she entered ministerial cabinets and government organizations in Belgium, her responsibilities ranging notably from equal opportunities to the international promotion of the cultural industries. Since 2010 she has been at the head of Wallonie-Bruxelles Architectures, an agency that ensures the international promotion of architects from the Wallonia-Brussels Federation.

Audrey Contesse is an art historian and architect. Currently the editor in chief of A+ Belgian Review of Architecture, she previously worked as an architect in several firms in Switzerland, the United States and Belgium. She also works as a critic and has notably published in Werk, bauen + wohnen, Bru, and L'Art Même. In 2009, she curated a series of films and lectures on the landscape and landscape architects in Belgium entitled 5/5 at ISELP, the Institut Supérieur d'Etude du Langage Plastique in Brussels. She was also one of the co-researchers on the Usus/Usures project for the Belgian pavilion at the 2010 Venice Architecture Biennale. She sits regularly on architecture juries for students and professionals.

Oswald Dellicour is a founding partner of Synergy International, a firm established in 1987. After graduating from the Institut Supérieur d'Architecture Saint-Luc (Brussels), he obtained a Master of Architecture degree from the Louis I. Kahn Studio programme at the University of Pennsylvania. With Synergy International he has been involved in architectural projects in Europe and Africa as well as South America and Asia. He received the Aga Kahn award in 1982 for the Nianing agricultural training centre in Senegal. For 30 years he has been a part-time lecturer at La Cambre school of architecture, now part of the University of Brussels (ULB). He has also been a visiting lecturer at Wits University in Johannesburg (2000-03) and has taken part in various conferences on architecture and appropriate technologies for developing countries.

Carl Destoop obtained masters' degrees in applied economic and commercial sciences from the Universities of Antwerp and Hasselt. This was later followed by a degree in interior design at the KH Mechelen. His main professional career started in 1994 at Flanders Investment & Trade. Over the years he has built up experience in several departments, notably getting involved in the internationalization of the creative industry, mostly design. Today he works in marketing, notably in branding Flanders through its creativity.

Daniel Dethier holds degrees in engineering and town planning. In 1992, he founded Dethier & Associés in Liège, which in 2010 became Dethier Architectures, and of which he is still the director. He has lectured at the University of Brussels (ULB) since 2005. His approach is defined by a critical vision that allows for innovative solutions in line with current needs in fields such as the typology of rural/urban housing, the valorization of building heritage, cultural infrastructure, urban planning, etc. From the start, the firm's projects have included a sustainable approach thanks to the attention paid to the durability of buildings. This key feature is discernible in both his early work and his latest projects, bringing new technologies into play for a minor environmental impact.

Daniel Dethier

Jean-Yves Del Forno

Kenneth Groosman

Pieter T'Jonck

Jean-Yves Del Forno graduated from the University of Liège in 1992 with a degree in civil engineering. He is currently one of the administrators of both Bureau Greisch and Greisch Ingénierie, where he now heads the bridges unit. He is also active as a scientific collaborator at the University of Liège. Since 1994 projects have included the E40-E25 link road at Liège (1994-2000), the Millau Viaduct (2000-2004), the railway bridge over the Garonne in Bordeaux (2005), the Oosterweel link in Antwerp (2005-2008), the bridge over the "Grande Ravine" on the island of Réunion (2006-2007) and the bridge over the "La Ravine Fontaine" on the same island (2001-2009).

Kenneth Groosman graduated as an architect from the Hoger Architectuurinstituut De Bijloke in 1991. From 1991 to 2005 he was active in several Ghent offices, where he worked on a lot of private commissions as well as on larger public works such as the Faculty of Veterinary Medicine of Ghent University. Active within the international multidisciplinary design company VK since 2006, he has worked on a wide range of hospital projects, among which OLVZ Aalst, UZ Brussels, and CHU Liège.

Pieter T'Jonck is an architect and art critic specializing in the fields of theatre, dance, architecture and, occasionally, fine arts. Besides heading the architectural firm T'Jonck-Nilis BV-BVBA, he has written for various media since 1980: Veto (1983-85), De Standaard (1985-2000), De Tijd (2001-06), De Morgen (since 2006), and Klara Radio (since 2006). He publishes regularly on the performing arts, architecture and urbanism in journals such as Etcetera, DWB, De Witte Raaf, Ballettanz (now Tanz), Springerin, Corpus AT and A+, and contributes to other book publications. In addition to architecture workshops at Ghent University (1994-2001), he has taught at the academy in Antwerp and Ghent. He is still involved with DasArts, Amsterdam as advisor and has run workshops on criticism in Amsterdam, Brussels, Istanbul, Vienna and Bucharest. He lives in Leuven.

Freek Persyn graduated from the Sint-Lukas Brussels University College of Art and Design in 1997. The following year he founded the architectural firm 51N4E with Peter Swinnen and Johan Anrys. In 2003, 51N4E was the recipient of the Rotterdam Maaskant Award for Young Architects. Next to his professional activities at 51N4E, he has been active in the academic world, currently as a visiting professor at the Academy of Architecture in Mendrisio, Switzerland. He regularly gives lectures in Belgium and abroad.

Christine de Ruijter studied architecture at the Henry Van de Velde Institute (Antwerp) and was a trainee at Valode et Pistre (Paris) and at AWG bOb van Reeth Architects. A professional architect since 1991, she was initially self-employed, before becoming a partner of the ArchitectsWorkGroup. Since 2002, she has been a founder and director of awg architecten. She has also acted as chairman of the Breda Building and Monument Commission, and been a member of the Antwerp Building Commission, Europan 9 judge, chairman of the Tilburg Building Commission, and Architect General for the village of Borsele. In education, too, she has had many roles, including: guest lecturer in architectural studies; visiting critic at the Delft University of

Freek Persyn

Christine de Ruijter

Ward Verbakel

Han Verschure

Technology; jury chairman and judge for student projects at the Sint-Lukas College of Arts & Sciences in Ghent; lecturer at the University of Liverpool; and Capita Selecta, Amsterdam Architecture Academy.

Ward Verbakel holds a degree in civil engineering and architecture from KULeuven. He studied at Columbia University in the Master of Science in Architecture and Urban Design programme. He co-founded plusoffice-architects in 2006. The Brussels-based practice in architecture, urbanism and design has worked on a wide range of projects, from landscape urbanism and master planning to residential and cultural projects. He is currently developing the master plan for a cluster of towns in Lommel and Landen, the redevelopment strategy for the Durance valley in France, and the park reconversion of a railyard in Essen. He teaches design studio at GSAPP Columbia University, KULeuven and in the European Master of Urbanism. His research for the KULeuven, UrbanResearchGroup and UN-Habitat focuses on urban voids and inhabited landscapes. A jury member for national architectural awards, he has lectured internationally and is a regular guest at architecture schools.

Han Verschure is professor emeritus with special assignments at KULeuven, active in the Postgraduate Centre Human Settlements (renamed MaHS MaUSP Centre). His specialties are training and capacity building, research, development and follow-up of projects in the habitat, spatial and environmental planning domains in developing countries. The programme director of the Master of Architecture in Human

Settlements (1985-2007), he has overseen many programmes for Belgian development aid and international agencies, including 'Localising Agenda 21: Strategic Planning for Sustainable Development'. He has chaired the working group on International Cooperation and Sustainable Development of the Federal Council for Sustainable Development, the Platform Local Agenda 21 of Leuven. An advisor for the UN Commissions on Human Settlements and the UN Commission Sustainable Development, he is active internationally as strategic planning advisor and teaches "Human Settlements in Development" at KULeuven.

Prudent de Wispelaere graduated from the University of Liège in 1977. He has been an associate architect at Charles Vandenhove & Associates since 1987. He has worked as co-architect on projects in Belgium (e.g., the Liège University Hospital, the urban renewal of Hors-Château in Liège, and the royal lodge of the opera house La Monnaie in Brussels), in the Netherlands (e.g., the courthouse in s'Hertogenbosch, the Royal Theatre in The Hague, the town hall in Ridderkerk, and housing projects in Amsterdam, Maastricht), and in France (e.g., the theatre Les Abesses, a dance school in Paris).

Jérôme Matthieu is business development manager at BPI SA (CFE Group). After seven years at the Brussels bar as a lawyer in commercial law, he entered the real estate business in 1999, first at CB Richard Ellis, then at Catella Codemer Belgium, one of the top three real estate agents on the Brussels market. He worked for the investment department and joined the board of directors in 2003, becoming

Prudent de Wispelaere

Jérôme Matthieu

Isidore Zielonka

managing director in 2004. He has led some of the biggest real estate transactions on the Brussels market, mainly with international investors or EU institutions (e.g., Madou Tower 40 000 m²; Bastion Tower 34 000 m²; Corporate Village 43 000 m²). After seven years of brokerage activities, he joined BPI, the property development unit of the CFE Group, in order to source, develop and commercialize office and residential projects. BPI is currently developing around 100 000 m² in Belgium and controls another 400 000 m².

Isidore Zielonka graduated in architecture from La Cambre school of architecture in 1966. He was a founding partner of SRZ in 1969, and, in 1989, of Art & Build (offices in Brussels, Paris, Luxembourg and Toulouse). He has been exporting Belgian architecture since 1976 to the following destinations: Saudi Arabia (housing), Florida (marina and housing), United Kingdom (TV studio), Italy (offices), Luxembourg (offices, space planning) and France (Agora building and DEQM in Strasbourg for the Council of Europe, offices, hospitals, shops, town planning). He has also worked on the Jacques Delors building in Brussels, Monsanto's headquarters, the University of Brussels library (ULB), as well as schools and housing projects.

special issue
Belgian Architecture Beyond Belgium
A+ BIMONTHLY ARCHITECTURAL REVIEW
21/3 rue Ernest Allardstraat — B-1000 Bruxelles
TEL +32 2 645 79 10 FAX +32 2 640 27 95
info@a-plus.be | www.a-plus.be

EDITORS | DESIGN
EDITOR **Audrey Contesse**
EDITORIAL STAFF **Thomas Jasper Martin,**
Géraldine Michat
DESIGN **Studio van Son**, Brussels
TRANSLATIONS **Gregory Ball**, Ghent
Patrick Lennon, Brussels
PROOFREADING **Patrick Lennon**, Brussels

AUTHORS
Gilles Béchet, Audrey Contesse, Johan Lagae,
Thomas Jasper Martin, Géraldine Michat,
Benjamin Pors, Pieter T'Jonck, Dieter Van Den Storm,
Christophe Van Gerrewey, Cécile Vandernoot

EDITORIAL ADVISERS
Goedele Desmet, Benoît Moritz

PUBLISHER
A+EDITIONS | ICASD vzw CIAUD asbl
Information Centre for Architecture,
Urban Development and Design
info@ciaud-icasd.be | www.ciaud-icasd.be
PRESIDENT **Leen Gysen**
VICE-PRESIDENT **Chantal Vincent**
SECRETARY **Kristiaan Borret**
administration@ciaud-icasd.be
SECRETARIAT **Benedicte Muls**
secretariat@ciaud-icasd.be

COPYRIGHT ICASD
The responsibility for published articles rests with
the authors. All rights of reproduction (even partly),
translation and editing are reserved for all countries.

RESPONSIBLE PUBLISHER
Leen Gysen
21/3 rue Ernest Allardstraat — B-1000 Bruxelles

PRINTED BY
Claes-Printing, Sint-Pieters-Leeuw

ADVERTISING A+MEDIA
Rita Minissi
TEL +32 2 332 37 82 FAX +32 2 332 37 83
rita.minissi@mima.be
21/3 rue Ernest Allardstraat — B-1000 Bruxelles
TEL +32 2 645 79 10 | FAX +32 2 640 27 95

BOOK LAUNCH
A+/BOZAR ARCHITECTURE
COORDINATOR **Iwan Strauven**
PROJECT LEADER **Marie-Cécile Guyaux**

SPONSORS
B&G | BEGA | BULEX | CLAES PRINTING |
HEWI | K.U. LEUVEN | MIPIM | MODULYSS |
PHILIPS | REALTY | SILESTONE | VELUX | VK GROUP

6000 copies of this issue were printed

ISBN 9789490814014
Legal deposit D/2012/2443/1

with the support of

With the support of
the Flemish authorities

FÉDÉRATION
WALLONIE-BRUXELLES

BRUSSELS
invest & export

Flanders **Investment & Trade**
Government of Flanders - Belgium

A+ BELGIAN REVIEW OF ARCHITECTURE

THE REFERENCE FOR ARCHITECTURE IN BELGIUM

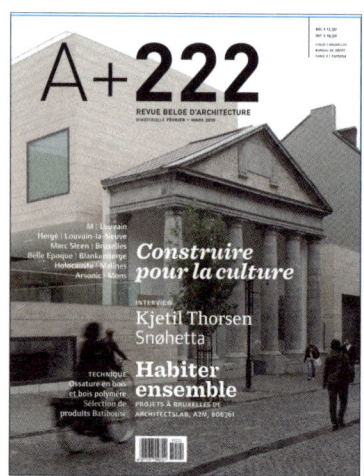

BELGIUM 65 € STUDENTS 49 € | EUROPE 95 € STUDENTS 79 € | WORLD 115 € STUDENTS 99 €

A+

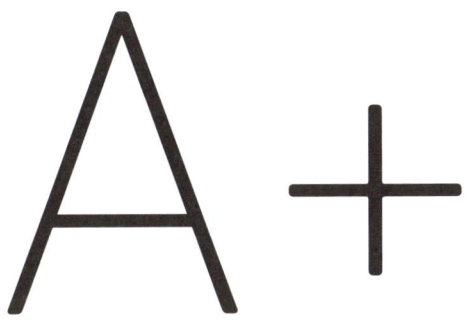

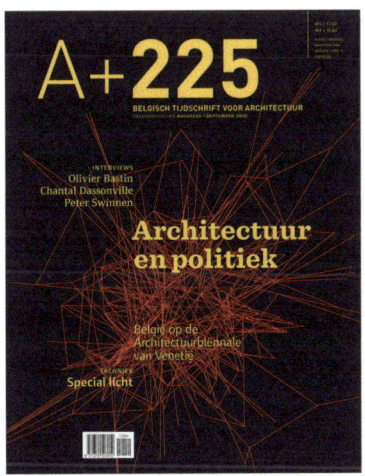

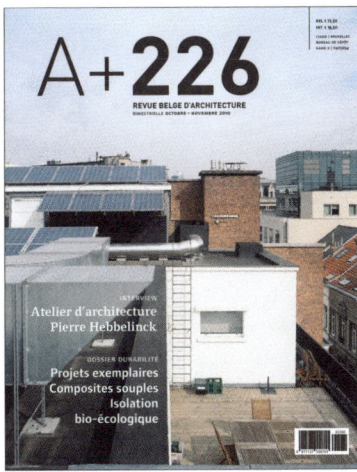

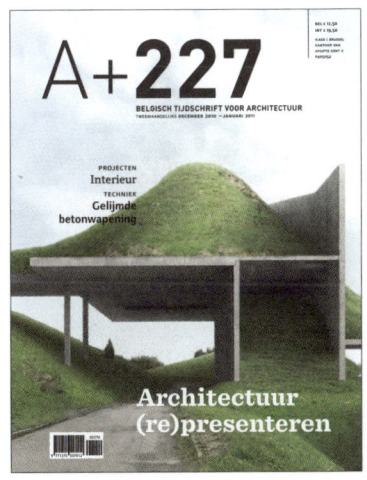

A STORY OF BIG NAMES?

published by A+Editions, Brussels | February 2012
printed by Claes-Printing, Sint-Pieters-Leeuw